Life Space Management

Life Space Management

By
P S Siwach

Vij Books India Pvt Ltd
New Delhi (India)

Published by

Vij Books India Pvt Ltd
(Publishers, Distributors & Importers)
2/19, Ansari Road
Delhi – 110 002
Phones: 91-11-43596460, 91-11-47340674
Fax: 91-11-47340674
e-mail: vijbooks@rediffmail.com

ISBN: 978-93-82652-85-4

ISBN Ebook : 978-93-82652-86-1

Dedicated To

My Parents Shri Giri Raj Singh & Shakuntla Devi

&

My Spiritual Guru Shri Shivrudrabalayogi

Contents

Preface

While constructing my house at Secunderabad (AP), I went to witness the laying of the first slab by the builder. The builder told me before laying the slab that if I wanted any minor changes to be made in my house it had to be done before starting the laying of the slab and no changes would be done after construction of the slab. Since my wife and self had discussed and changed so many designs of the house there was a lingering doubt in my mind whether the house I was constructing would meet my full requirements or would it fall short of it. Sometimes I also had a feeling that the house I was building might be too big for me to maintain in my old age. With these doubts in my mind I climbed the roof top of my neighbour's house to witness the laying of the ground floor slab. It was a hectic activity that I was witnessing. While my doubt was still disturbing me whether the space I was building was adequate or not, I observed a small semi nude urchin a child of one of the labourers fast asleep on a gunny sack right in middle of the hectic activity that was going on. On seeing the child I laughed at myself for being so confused and uncomfortable with the space I was building; here very before my eyes slept a kid who just needed 2'*2' of space and was most comfortable in that space. Also I thought of his parents who must have built so many palatial houses while they lived in a make shift shelter made of plastic sheet for a roof. Next day I discussed this dilemma with my colleague then a Colonel and now retired Lt Gen BK Chengappa. 'Chengs', as he was popularly known very casually told me "Pradeep life is nothing but a struggle for space." These pearls of wisdom appealed to my inner conscience and that triggered my quest for research on this subject. During the course of my study I came across the word life space coined by Kurt Lewin.

I found that life space as such had not been adequately researched and life space management certainly had no literature available. I found the subject intriguing and interesting. Though life and space both had been researched and analysed in great depth by various sciences and intellectuals yet it remained an enigma worth exploring. I therefore sought the views of my spiritual Guru Shri Shivrudrabalayayogi. He in a very simple manner explained and guided me to understand both about life and space and its relevance to our existence.

After my research I tried to experiment in my own small way whether the theory that I had worked on had a pragmatic application or not. To my joy I found it works. It has brought about a massive change in my life. I am able to connect with people better.

If this theory of life space management has worked for me I am sure it will work for you too. After all life is all about exploring and experimenting with new ideas and concepts.

I wish you all become huge creators of life space in the environment. May your name fame and glory become eternal.

- Brigadier Pradeep Singh Siwach (Retd)

Acknowledgement

At the outset, I whole heartedly express my deep sense of gratitude to my Supervisor, Dr Vanka Sita, Professor, School of Management Studies, Central University Hyderabad, who was a constant source of inspiration in execution of this research work from the beginning to end. But for her guidance, encouragement and help my thesis could not have been completed. She inspired me to convert my thesis "Application of Life Space Management a comparative study between Defence and Civil Organaisations"into this book.

I am also thankful to the respondents of the study area, from defence services, academics and industry across the country, for their kind cooperation in data collection.

I would be failing in my duty, if I do not place on record my gratitude to my Spiritual Guru Shri Shivrudrabalyogi for the moral support and guidance provided for the study, without which I could not have achieved anything. I also owe my gratitude to my parents who have always been a source of inspiration to me.

I owe my thanks to all others who have helped me in my journey of research. I am grateful to my PA Sandeep Sharma who has helped me in compiling my book. My wife Alka and daughters Priyanka and Samiksha deserve a mention for putting up with me during the course of this study

- Brigadier Pradeep Singh Siwach (Retd)

Chapter 1

Introduction

Every human being is born with a specific purpose. One of the main purposes of human existence is to be an effective part of a family, group, society or organization. No human being can exist in isolation. A man living in isolation will alienate the individual from human condition and thus deprive the individual from human living environment and experiential learning. (Zimbardo. Ebbesen, Maslach, 1977). The relevance of purpose is not fully comprehended by vast majority and they waste a full life time in trying to define or find out the purpose of their existence. In Mahabharat it is mentioned that even Lord Krishna had told Arjuna that everything in this universe is created for a purpose. He had told him when Arjuna wept on seeing his dearest chariot burn and reduce to ashes after the great battle of Mahabharata was over. The great chariot was gifted to Arjuna by Agni Deva (diety of fire) and same got burnt because its purpose for which it was created was achieved and it was no longer required. (Kamala Subramanium, 2004). As per Sri Manibhai (1998), man in his present form, lives in a state of ignorance. He has no true goal of life and wastes his whole life driven by passions and endless desires. Man is a very complex living being gifted with faculty of an independent mind and thinking process. Yet that intellect is not fully utilized to define the purpose of one's existence.

The greatest challenge in any organisation or walk of life is to understand human behaviour especially in a work environment. Study of human behaviour in the work environment covers more than just the activities involved with the actual work. There are several other variables that influence and generate formal and informal interactions that have an impact on human behaviour. (Francis & Milbourn Jr,1980).Families, societies, and organizations are all made up of people. The real life energy in these small and big social systems is dependent on the human beings only; as by themselves they are nothing. The characteristics of these social and professional systems are an outcome of collective characteristics of the individuals who are part of these systems. Before one understands the characteristics of organizations one must understand individual human behaviour. Human behaviour is complex and unpredictable. So much of research work has been carried out on study of human behaviour, and yet there is no definite theory that is complete in itself to define human behaviour. Human beings not only come in various shapes and sizes but also behave in exceedingly complex ways. Psychology, sociology, anthropology, astrology, theology, philosophy, literature and life sciences represent some of the many means taken to understand the complexity of human existence and behaviour. (Hjelle and Ziegler, 1992).

Human beings are social animals. They are referred to as social animals because man is constantly interacting with other men. (Lawless, 1972). They come together for common good. It is said that modern world is a world of organizations. Etzioni (1965) writes, "We are born in organizations, educated by organizations, and most of us spend much of our lives working for organizations." Rao & Narayana (2000) quote Hicks and Gullet (1975) and explain that people organize for three material reasons: first to enlarge abilities, second to compress the time required to accomplish an objective and third to take advantage of the accumulated knowledge of previous generation. In these organizations the prime responsibility of management should be development of human resource. People first and not things first should be the approach of management; as management of man is most critical and important for survival of an organization. (Ravishankar & Mishra, 1994). In nearly all organisations there is a direct link between the effectiveness of individual employees in their role and the overall effectiveness and profitability, of the organisation. It is therefore management's responsibility to ensure that they create an environment whereby employees continually become more effective at what they do. Managers need to help them understand how they should perform the role by identifying any gaps in their skills, knowledge and experience and providing training and other development opportunities to cover the new areas. Individuals need opportunities to take new skills learned in an offline environment and adopt them into routine behaviour in the workplace. This process can be hastened by skilled use of coaching and mentoring, as also making employees understand that the entire effectiveness of the organization depends on the collective effectiveness of the individuals. The entire growth of the organization is dependent on the effectiveness of the organization. The more effective it is the more life space it creates in the environment. Similarly in our daily lives at individual level; the amount of life space we create in the environment is a reflection of our effectiveness. This life space needs to be managed, to enhance our effectiveness.

Chapter 2

The Concept and Its Application

Every human being aspires to do well in life. It is an inherent desire that each human being posses. Certain ramifications of this desire manifest themselves through various acts and motives to present a picture of effectiveness in the desired field. Presentation of this picture of effectiveness and perfection is nothing but a representation of an effort to create the right space by an individual in the environment.

Human beings continuously spend a lot of time and energy to create the right space in the environment that they live in. This aspect of creation of space is an abstract concept that each individual practices without being aware of it. If this is an issue that is vigorously pursued by each individual then there is a need to understand how this should be managed to further enhance the effectiveness of individuals.

Is this concept applicable to human beings or does it have a universal application. If one closely observes the behavioural pattern of organisations and nations one comes to the conclusion that the behavioural pattern of these entities is a mere reflection of the sum total behaviour of the people of the organisation/ nation. This behaviour pattern is deeply influenced by the behavioural pattern of the leadership and the led. Since behaviour of these entities is a mere reflection of human behaviour, it is observed that even organisations and nations struggle for space and their entire effectiveness is dependent upon how well they manage to create the right space in the environment.

The corporate wars between competing rivals are the norm of the day. Bigger and modern industries have forced smaller industries to wind up their shop as they are not able to sustain themselves in a competitive environment. With the opening of Indian markets to global auto industry,

Fiat and Ambassador Cars in India which ruled the roost during licence raj have suddenly become a thing of the past. Closure of several cottage industries in India reflects this competitive environment. Also dumping of cheap goods by developing/ developed nations has speeded up the closure of several industries the world over. Marketing strategies are all designed to create the right space with their present and potential customers and other stake holders. Pepsi and Coke turf wars are globally known. Mature industries do believe in win - win situations by dividing the territories of operation in an amicable way. Those industries which did not understand the relevance of creating the right space with their stake holders have either perished or are on the verge of closing down.

Similarly in politics and in media we read and hear comments on how India and Pakistan are vying with each other to create space with United States of America. Smaller nations struggle and compete with each other to create space with stronger nations for their survival. Even in the animal kingdom animals mark their territories and strongly guard them.

Lebensraum (living space) is a Nazi German word, which is a reflection of the struggle for space between nations. Though the geopolitical concept of lebensraum became popular during Hitler's regime it was however coined by Friedrich Ratzel in the late nineteenth century. It was used as a slogan in Germany referring to the unification of the country and the acquisition of colonies, as per the English and French models. Ratzel propounded that the development of people is primarily influenced by their geographical situation, and that people that successfully adapted to one location would proceed naturally to another. This expansion to fill available space, he claimed, was a natural and necessary feature of any healthy species. These beliefs were furthered by scholars of the day, including Karl Haushofer and Friedrich von Bernhardi. Von Bernhardi's in his book written in 1912 'Germany and the Next War', expanded upon Ratzel's hypotheses, and, for the first time, explicitly identified Eastern Europe as a source of new space for Germany. Adolf Hitler gave a practical dimension to lebensraum by expanding the boundaries of Germany as he mentioned in in his book ' Mein Kampf' that Germany as a world power could not be confined to an absurd area of five hundred thousand square kilometers. While Germany at the end of Second World War became infamous for adapting lebensraum as a state policy, lebensraum today is practiced by all developing nations in nearly every field, be it economic, culture, defence, energy etc. Overthrow of regime in Afghanistan and invasion of Iraq post 9/11, twisting the arm of North Korea and Iran by US and her allies using nuclear proliferation as a theme is a physical manifestation of lebensraum in the present global environment. Invasion of culture through media is the invisible aspect of lebensraum exercised by the developed on helpless and developing nations.

In the fraternity of cosmologists there is a belief that, in space there are several other universes spatially finite, like our universe which is all jostling for space with each other. Andre Linde, a cosmologist, mentions recent versions of inflationary scenario that describes the universe as a self generating fractural that sprouts other inflationary universe. An aspect that cosmologists theorize about universe is that they are dynamic and self reproducing. If universes are self reproducing then they are also growing and if they are growing then they will need more and more space.

In fact struggle for space is cosmic and universal in nature. Struggle for space starts from the smallest element and this has been scientifically validated.

The universe we live in has one fundamental property, it is expanding. This property is known as the 'Hubble Flow' after the scientist Edwin Hubble. Anything that is expanding will require more and more space.

Even human beings attempt to expand in their chosen fields. In a given environment, space is finite; therefore individual human beings, organisations, nations and universes in their attempt to expand encroach upon others space. This encroachment of space is also a struggle for survival. Darwinian Theory espouses survival of the fittest implying an aggressive attitude of human behaviour wherein the human being wants to control the environment by possessing the environment. In their quest to control the environment there is a constant struggle for space at all levels i.e. individual, organisational and national level. Sri Aurobindo (1970) too supplements this view , " The struggle for life is not only a struggle to survive, it is also a struggle for possession and perfection, since only by taking hold of the environment whether more or less, whether by self-adaptation to it or by adapting it to oneself either by accepting and conciliating it or by conquering and changing it, can survival be secured, and equally it is true that only greater and greater perfection can assure a continuous permanence, a lasting survival". Struggle for space therefore is a cosmic phenomenon, which is practiced by all.

The phenomenon would consist of certain root parameters which if managed or applied well would enhance effectiveness of an individual, an organisation or a nation. From a general observation it is evident that managing life space is an intrinsic nature with human beings as they continue to practice the same subconsciously. In the field of management this aspect is not well documented, though several researches on basic parameters of life space have been carried out by various philosophers, psychologists and behavioural scientists.

Chapter 3

What is Life Space

What is life space needs to be understood in greater detail before analysis of its application. Life Space is a term which has been coined by Kurt Lewin a charismatic US psychologist of German origin. Lewin is known as the founder of modern psychology in the field of human behaviour. The development of his field theory which propounds that human behaviour is the function of both the person and the environment expressed in symbolic terms, B= f(P,E). To elaborate it would emerge that in a given situation S (i.e., a particular person P in a particular environment E) have the event B and no other as a result? This question is answered if we succeed in discovering the dynamic structure of the situation in question. As per Kurt Lewin the cause of the event consists in the properties of the momentary life space or of certain integral parts of it.

Kurt Lewin's field theory has its roots in Gestalt theory. (A gestalt is a coherent whole. It has its own laws, and is a construct of the individual mind rather than 'reality'). As per Lewin a field is defined as 'the totality of coexisting facts which are conceived of as mutually interdependent'. The whole psychological field has been defined as 'life space' by Kurt Lewin. As per him it is 'life space', within which people act. In order to understand human behaviour one must understand the dynamics of life space. Psychological field is generally abstract. Kurt Lewin tried to represent it in mathematical terms by drawing its boundaries in topological terms by drawing maps of the various psychological fields. If we are to accomplish the task of deriving the behaviour of the person (in more general terms: the psychological events) from the life space, we have to characterize it as the "totality of possible events."

What is meant by psychological life space and what must one take into consideration in order to represent it? While psychological life space is abstract in nature it is influenced by the physical and social environment in which the individual exists. Therefore one will have to understand the physical and social environment of the individual that are important for him at the given moment. Physical environment can be represented by his residence, workplace, town or country; while social environment can be represented by relationships to other persons, their positions and personalities, and his own place in society. At the same time, his longings and ambitions will also play an important role including his fears, thoughts, ideals, and daydreams, in short everything that from the standpoint of the psychologist exists for this person. It is, however, not always easy to determine what things exist psychologically for a given person. The most obvious method might seem to be the use of consciousness as a criterion. This would mean that the physical and social environment would be treated as psychological environment in so far as the person is conscious of them.

- Victor Daniel (2005) agrees with Kurt Lewin, that life space is determined by the environment and the people one is in association with. Life space according to him includes: two dimensions one of physical existence and the other of mental existence. He elaborates it by saying, "When you're planning what to do tomorrow, your life-space is not the room you're in now but the place where you expect to be tomorrow. Your present locomotion in that expected environment involves deciding on one course of action rather than another, as a result of vectors that impel you in one or another direction." Perceptions deeply influence these vectors.

- Within this individuals and groups can be identified in topological terms (using map-like representations). Individuals participate in a series of life spaces (such as the family, work, society), and these were constructed under the influence of various force vectors.

It is felt that life space as defined by Kurt Lewin is restrictive therefore to further understand Life Space and its management it is better to define and understand the two rudimentary elements of life space i.e. Life and Space in greater detail for that would help clarify what constitutes life space.

Chapter 4

Defining Life

Perceptions about life vary from individual to individual. Though all have an idea and rudimentary understanding of life yet no one can give any one definition to life, for life emerges as varied as the preceptor of life. It is therefore very difficult to have a universal definition of life. Life is defined in different connotations by various authors and scientists. Definition of life as given by a biologist will vary in content from that of a philosopher and so on. One can understand the deeper meaning of life without taking a holistic approach. This would be possible by analysing the meaning of life as spelt out in various sciences and by various personalities from different perspectives.

Biological Viewpoint

As per Wikipedia free encyclopedia "Life is a multi-faceted concept. Life may refer to the ongoing process of which living things are a part; the period between the birth (or a point at which the entity can be considered to be living) and death of an organism; the condition of an entity that has been born (or reached the point in its existence at which it can be established to be alive) and has yet to die; and that which makes a living thing alive." A conventional biological definition as per Wikipedia free encyclopedia mentions that an entity may be considered to be alive if it exhibits growth, metabolism, motion, reproduction and response to stimuli. Similar views have been expressed in *'The American Heritage Stedman's Medical Dictionary', which describes that t*he property or quality that distinguishes living organisms from dead organisms and inanimate matter, is manifested in functions such as metabolism, growth, reproduction, and response to stimuli or adaptation to the environment originating from within the organism. An analysis of these conventional definitions reveals certain inherent drawbacks in these definitions. As per these definitions fire can be classified as having life as it moves responds and grows. Similarly a mule or an ant would be classified as non living as they do not reproduce. Modern biology explains life, living beings, as a highly organized material entities composed of cells composed of molecules and as results of a long process of evolution by ripe with emergent structure.

Another biological view and definition of life has been given by Haboku Nakamura - Biology Institute, Konan University, Kobe, Japan, as "Living beings are systems that have three simultaneous features: they are self-supported, they reproduce themselves and they evolve through interaction with the environment." Further Sidney Fox of South Alabama University, USA , speaks of living beings as protein-made bodies formed by one or more cells that communicate with the environment through information transfer carried out by electric impulses or chemical substances, and capable of morphological evolution and metabolism, growth and reproduction.

Anything that is born must die is a universal truth. Therefore life is the state of being which begins with generation, birth, or germination, and ends with death. The time during which this state continues; that state of an animal or plant in which all or any of its organs are capable of performing all or any of their functions; used of all animal and vegetable organisms can described as the period of life.

Anthropologist View

These days, a popular definition of what it means to be alive is to say that 'life' is a chemical system that can undergo Darwinian evolution. This sounds pretty good since Darwinian evolution is certainly fundamental to all terrestrial life.

Philosophical View

Camilo J. Cela-Conde of Dept. of Philosophy, University of Baleares mentions that living beings are able to elaborate information in such a way that in the sequence "environmental stimulus - construction of knowledge - motor response", the possible results in terms of input that cannot be mechanically predicted.

Helen Keller writes "Life is a daring adventure or nothing. To keep our faces toward change and behave like free spirits in the presence of fate is strength undefeatable." Theun Mares writes in his book 'The Mists Of Dragon Lore' "Life for the average man and woman is nothing more than a dream, and their actions nothing more than folly. And yet this does not imply that life is not real, or that it cannot be real, nor does it imply that our actions are useless. What this aphorism does imply is that life is not what men and women believe it to be, and that if we base our actions on this false sense of reality, then our actions must perforce amount to folly."

"Life is like music," said Lazcano , "you can describe it but not define." And as in the case of time and music, the challenge to define life persists.

Life seems to evolve - evolution in consciousness, physical / mental / emotional / spiritual evolution. - from dense matter to lighter matter, from within without and thus life seems to obey certain laws - Natural laws, Universal laws, Physical laws, Newton's gravity laws and cause and affect etc. In human beings this evolution of life can be extended to the union of the soul and body; also, the duration of their union; sometimes, the deathless quality or existence of the soul; as, man is a creature having an immortal life.

Temporal

Temporal dimension to life has been added by physict Ayashlom C Ilitzur, who describes life as a process by which a spatio-temporal pattern, existing in a multitude of places and times, becomes a causal agent by itself. It is liberated of the constraints of its material medium, thereby interacting not only with the local, random aspects of the environment, but, also increasingly, with the invariant spatio-temporal regularities underlying it, namely, physical laws themselves

An Indian View

Sri Aurobindo the renowned freedom fighter and saint of India explained the highest ideals of life. He wrote about mind as a creative cosmic agency. He further elaborated that there is a subconscious mind in the force and matter which is at work which is responsible for its own emergence and for the emergence of forms of life and mind itself. He also mentioned about a constant dynamic energy in movement in the universe which takes various material forms and is stored and active as a constant dynamic force which we associate with the idea of life. He summed up life in the following words, " Life then is the dynamic play of a universal Force, a force in which mental consciousness and nervous vitality are in some form or at least in their principle always inherent and therefore they appear and organise themselves in our world in the form of Matter." Sri Aurobindo (1970).

Defining life is a futile effort; is very common among biologists, even though this complete and unreflective refusal of the very question does not constitute standard view. Most scientists are extremely skeptical toward attempts to make clear definitions of living beings - their objects of study. They simply assert (with some justification) that a definition is of no use in solving the various experimental puzzles of normal research. Claus Emmeche mentions that in a DNA lab or a molecular biology department, or in a research seminar, if one were to ask about what definition of life the researcher takes as his or her point of departure, one will be met with an indulgent smile.

Astrobiology Magazine sought out expert opinion on this important question from Dr. Carol Cleland, who teaches philosophy at Colorado University in Boulder and is a member of NASA's Astrobiology Institute. She shared her thoughts on the power of definitions to shape science and philosophy. She argued that it is a mistake to try to define "life." Such efforts reflect fundamental misunderstandings about the nature and power of definitions.

Definitions tell us about the meanings of words in our language, as opposed to telling us about the nature of the world. In the case of life, scientists are interested in the nature of life; they are not interested in what the word "life" happens to mean in the language. What really needed is to focus on coming up with an adequately general theory of living systems, as opposed to a definition of "life." But in order to formulate a general theory of living systems, one needs more than a single example of life. As revealed by its remarkable biochemical and microbiological similarities, life on Earth has a common origin. Despite its amazing morphological diversity, terrestrial life represents only a single case. The key to formulating a general theory of living systems is to explore alternative possibilities for life. It would be interesting in formulating a strategy for searching for extraterrestrial life that allows one to push the boundaries of our earth-centric concepts of life.

One thing almost everyone would agree on is that life is a complex phenomenon, with many facets that emerge only after careful examination. (Joseph Morales, 1998), yet it is notoriously difficult to say what exactly is life. Many like Taylor, Farmer and Belin (1992) have put across similar view point. Also there seems to be no single property that characterizes life. Any property that we assign to life is either too broad, so that it characterizes many nonliving systems as well, or too specific, so that we can find counter-examples that we intuitively feel to be alive, but that do not satisfy it. The fact today is that we know of no set of individually necessary and jointly sufficient conditions for life. Mark A Bedau proposes that an automatic and continually creative evolutionary process of adapting to changing environments is the primary form of life.

From study of all definitions of life as enunciated by various people it emerges that all definitions fall short as they do not cover all aspects of life and are thus restrictive in nature. Life as a creative evolutionary process as is generally understood by all is considered for this study.

Chapter 5

Understanding Space

The vastness of space seems beyond comprehension therefore space has also been defined as the unlimited expanse in which everything is located. It is also defined as an interval between two times. Absolute space is defined as physical space independent of what occupies it. Space and time are thus interrelated and need to be studied as such. As everything in this universe exists in space, various dimensions of space thus need to be studied and analysed to comprehend the relevance of space in our lives. Space itself has been defined in different terms based on how space is construed and perceived in its various dimensions. Holistic understanding of space in its various dimensions will thus give a more comprehensive insight of space which is relevant for this study. Some of these dimensions of space are enumerated in succeeding paragraphs:-

Physical space

Space as is visible, felt and comprehended is a mere reflection of the physical space. In this physical space one experiences one's own existence and the existence of the environment. This physical environment consists of various activity centers like house, work place, markets and communication means etc. This can also be labeled as the existential space. This existential space has a great influence on human behaviour. Existential space combines an experience of space with a remaking of the space of the lived world. Both these activities are largely without formal conceptualization. In contrast, architecture space is also founded on spatial experience involved in a deliberate attempt to create spaces in the environment.

Environment thus becomes an activity space – originally a physical space but now days with proliferation of information technology even virtual spaces qualify as activity spaces; which are well populated with resources, tools and restrictions in which a living being operates. Same physical space can support multiple environments or activity spaces. A simple fact is that there is more to activity spaces than mere physical presence. Every environment simultaneously represents a space of possibility and a set of constraints. An environment is thus the space in which structures are created and actions have consequences. A very important facet of work environment therefore is that it constrains both what is possible or acceptable to do, and what happens as a result of performing actions. It is partly the product of projections and partly the product of underlying causal realities.

Relationships between space and human activity are thus very intricate and implicit; since it is where our actions take place. 'Place' is defined in anthropological terms as a space that has acquired meaning as a result of human activities. Academicians have advocated for talking about place rather than space: "Space is the opportunity; place is the understood reality" wrote Harrison and Dourish (1996). They further clarified that "a place is invested with understandings of behavioural appropriateness, cultural expectations, and so forth. "We are located in space but we act in place." (Harrison and Dourish, 1996). Erickson (1993) sums up this by stating that "Place is Space with Meaning". Nicholas Nova (2003) further quoting Harrison and Dourish mentions that by building up a history of experiences, space becomes a "place" and then its significance and utility is put forward, as a medium for significant actions. Place affords a kind of activity. While place is more specific, space is more generic in nature and encompasses other elements of nature like time etc. Erickson claims that spatial constraints can generate activity; he takes the example of the pedestrians who while waiting at crossroads for the light to change, sometimes study the headlines of news paper and perhaps decide to buy it. The physical space within which one lives and moves has a very great effect on a person's life. In residential care physical space is a very important factor in everything that occurs or is planned. (Maier. H.W., 2000),

Joiner mentions that another aspect of physical and virtual spaces is that they are not empty. Objects and things occupy places and hence do have a certain state and location, which is subject to change and modification. Each artifact in the environment has thus a role in social interaction by itself or by its modification. That is why, relationships between artifacts and space allows us to define different functions. To broaden the view, there are a lot of examples of formal situations where spatial relationships between people and objects are used to reinforce social distinctions and thus to mould the kinds of social interaction to be expected within the spaces. (Nicolas Nova, September 2003).

"Proximity helps people to relate people to activities and to each other." (Harrison and Dourish, 1996). In examining the impact of inter-relation between place/space and social interaction, an interesting result is that physical settings, constraints, social interactions and conversely those interactions modify space. (Nicolas Nova, September 2003). The way people stand or are seated thus appears to influence the interaction patterns of the group (Hare & Bales, 1963). A study of proxemics by Edward T Hall too reveals the same. The simplest example is that in a gathering, participants of a group generally welcome one into the group by repositioning themselves to form a circle thereby including the new member. Division of labour is another social function supported by spatiality. Indeed, Harrison and Dourish (1996) state that "distance can be used to partition activities and the extent of interaction". These details have been amply elaborated later while dealing with the subject of proxemics.

Sir Isaac Newton regarded absolute and real space in the sense of Euclidean geometry. According to Newton, space was a self-subsistent reality, a container inside which all objects are placed; it was as per him "God's boundless uniform sensorium." (Pinhas Ben- Zvi, Internet, November 2005). Space, in Euclidean Geometry, is a concept which is independent of the attributes of our human minds and senses. The word Geometry is derived from Greek words; *geo* "earth", and *metron* "to measure", namely "earth measurement". With such semantic-conceptual roots Pinhas Ben- Zvi further elaborates that its hardly conceivable that Euclid regarded Geometry as divorced from an objective independent space. Space being all encompassing cannot be viewed in Euclidean Geometry terms alone. This would mean that a larger meaning of space be understood.

Psychological Space

Psychological space though basically a figure of speech is a conceptual metaphor which connects or fuses the two conceptual unrelated domains of Psyche and Space, or Mind and Body, or Spirit and Matter.

If one is accustomed to speak of psychological facts as something essentially non spatial, one thinks first of physical space. An essential characteristic of this physical space is that it is thought of as a single coherent space which includes the totality of all physical facts that exist at a certain time in this whole physical world. . The facts of psychology, i.e. , these facts which psychology must recognize as real, have, according to the teaching of physics, no place within physical space. This is equally true of economic or aesthetic or other facts.

In consequence of this revolutionary assertion Kant states that: "Space is not an empirical concept which has been derived from outer experiences." On the contrary: "…it is the subjective condition of sensibility, under which alone outer intuition is possible for us." This would imply that the physical and social environment would be treated as psychological environment in so far as the person is conscious of them. Such a formulation is however doubtful, even if one uses the concept of consciousness in a very broad manner.

While talking of psychological space George Kellys work deserves to be studied in detail. He was a clinical psychologist who lived between 1905 and 1967. He published a two volume work, defining 'Personal construct psychology' in 1955, and went on to publish a large number of papers further developing his theory. Personal construct psychology is akin to a later coined term 'cognitive science'. Kelly presented his theory as geometry of psychological space and his conceptual framework is very clear if seen in these terms. Mildred L G Shaw & Brain R Gains(October 1992) while eulogizing Kelly reflect that Kelly's use of geometry was an intentional logic; one in which predicates are defined in terms of their properties rather than extensionally in terms of those entities that fall under them. Kelly as per them introduces the notion of a psychological space as a term for a region in which one may place and classify elements of ones experience. It is important to note that he did not suppose this space to pre-exist as a world of such elements, but rather to come into being through a process of construction by which one creates a space in which to place elements as one comes to construe them. He sees others as creating dimensions in personal psychological space as a way of providing a coordinate system for their experience, and emphasizes that the topology of the space comes into existence as it is divided: Kelly's work cannot be seen in isolation. He seems to have been influenced by Kurt Lewin's work. For both have tried to build and relate these experiences of life that influence human behaviour by mapping them into topological patterns. To understand human behaviour Kelly postulated a few terms, main ingredients of which are as given below:-

(a) A person's processes are psychologically channelised by the way in which he anticipates events. And he anticipates these events by construing their replications from past experiences.

(b) Man looks at his world through transparent templates which he creates and then attempts to fit over the realities of which the world is composed.

(c) Constructs are used for predictions of things to come, and the world keeps on rolling on and revealing these predictions to be either correct or misleading. This fact provides the basis for the revision of constructs and, eventually, of whole constructs systems. The construct is a basis of making a distinction...not a class of objects, or an abstraction of a class, but a dichotomous reference axis.

(d) A construct is convenient for the anticipation of a finite range of events only. A personal construct system can hardly be said to have universal utility. Not everything that happens in the world can be projected upon all the dichotomies that make up a person's outlook. The geometry of the mind is never a complete system.

(d) Our psychological geometry is geometry of dichotomies. "A person's construction system is composed of a finite number of dichotomous constructs."(Mildred L G Shaw & Brain R Gains, October 1992).

Kelly's geometry of psychological space thus gives personal construct psychology strong theoretical foundations. Personal construct psychology provides foundations for cognitive science and artificial intelligence that are consistent with current positions in these disciplines, but supplies an integrative framework that is currently lacking. Mildred L G Shaw & Brain R Gains(October 1992) further elaborate that personal construct psychology is a theory of individual and group psychological and social processes that has been used extensively in knowledge acquisition research to model the cognitive processes of human experts. It therefore has a great relevance to understanding human behaviour.

Cognitive Space

Cognitive space is a derivative of psychological space. Cognitive space uses the analogy of location in two, three or higher dimensional space to describe and categorize the thoughts, memories and ideas. Each individual has his/her cognitive space, resulting in a unique categorization of their ideas. The dimensions of this cognitive space depend on information, training and finally on a person's awareness. All this is deeply influenced by the cultural setting that an individual is functioning/ living in.

Cognitive space like psychological space consists of the abstract construct of space derived from the identification of space as an object for contemplation or reflection and the attempt to develop theories about it. The essence of this kind of space lies in the relative location of things.. In other words, Kant asserts that space (and time) is not objective, self-subsisting realities, but subjective requirements of our human sensory-cognitive faculties to which all things must conform. Space and time serve as indispensable tools that arrange and systemize the images of the objects imported by our sensory organs. The raw data supplied by our sensory organs like eyes and ears would be useless if our minds did not have space and time to make sense of it all.

Just as modern physicists speak of space and time as being two elements or aspects of the same seamless whole – space time -- so narrative psychologists analyze individual human lives as they unfold in psychological "space time". In the narrative approach, psychological "time" and psychological "space" are viewed, of course, not in the objective impersonal manner of the physicist, but in a subjective, fashion: through the eyes of the individual person whose life is being considered, as individual sees it, through his or her individual frame of reference. These frames of reference are deeply influenced by the socio-cultural environment in which one grows up in.

Social Space

Social space is a concept developed by Donald Black and used to explain the behavior of social life- such as law and order, art, terrorism and science. This space is created by social interaction, and its shape is defined by the social characteristics of those involved in the interaction. The shape of social space its topology in physical terms predicts and explains social life.Social space is defined as an inter subjective matrix of psychological distances based on physical and social reality that provides a framework constraining how people are influenced by each other. (Bibb Latane, 1996), Social space can be categorised into five dimensions as given below:-

(a) **The Normative Dimension:** It is defined by the application of social controls   e.g. Persons with criminal records, have a low position in this dimension.

(b) **The Vertical Dimension:** It is defined by the distribution of material wealth.

(c) **The Corporate Dimension:** It is distinguished by the capacity for collective action i.e. organization.

(d) **The Horizontal Dimension:** It is defined by the distribution of individuals in relation to one another (such as intimacy and integration).

(e) **The Symbolic Dimension:** It is defined by the differences in the amount and content of culture.

Bibb Latane, (1996), mentions that social space is built considering the traces of human actions left in the environment by people. Every living organism sends signals into social space that can be decoded by others. These signals create an imprint in the social environment. Dieberger (1999) points out that social connotation may influence specific communication patterns in space. Different patterns of communication occur in various environments between various social interactions. Space modifies communication patterns among people. Social space when it firms up over a long period of time leads to the creation of a culture.

Cultural Space

The most capacious space within which we think about ourselves is called culture. Culture is not easy to define. The Dictionary of the History of Ideas refers to 164 of such definitions. Elvin Hatch in Adam and Jessica Kuper's "The Social Science Encyclopedia" defines culture as a way of life of a people. It consists of conventional patterns of thought and behaviour, including values, beliefs, rules of conduct, political organisation, economic activity, and the like, which are passed on from one generation to the next by learning - and not by biological inheritance. The concept of culture is an idea of great significance, for it provides a set of principles for explaining and understanding human behaviour. It is one of the distinguishing elements of modern social thought, and may be one of the most important achievements of modern social science, and in particular of anthropology.

Cultural space is created by cultural activities of a society or civilization. This space not only locates core cultural meanings with regard to each other, but also locates each culture on the basis of its profile. In real world even abstracts like culture too need space to grow and nurture (Dipankar Gupta, 2000). Furthermore, cultures will cluster together in this space as they share common languages, philosophy, religion, and so on. At the most general level, we can discern three major clusters in this global cultural space. The first defines those largely Western cultures, which is basically represented by American; a materialistic culture in which religion plays a relatively minor role; philosophy is of the empirical pragmatic variety; with considerable emphasis on science, especially empirical-experimental science. Their core comprises sensory meanings and values; their criterion of truth is empirical. Thus there is empiricism, the hedonism, the utilitarianism and the concern with individual liberty. While there exists diminutive role of religion, metaphysics, theory and intuition, reason, and ethico-legal systems all emphasize eternal values and ultimate truths.

The second cluster of cultures lies in an opposite region of cultural space. Religion and metaphysical philosophies dominate, science is speculative and theoretical; ethics stresses dissolving the self into a greater whole, of transcending sensual delights for eternal truths; art tries to capture the unchanging. This can be equated with the Oriental culture. The third variety is primitive lacking both in science and sound philosophy and ethics. A large component of such culture is below the level of conscious awareness.

Also cultural patterns structure both thought and perception. Modern thinking about culture is in some ways consistent with psychoanalytic ideas. It is now understood that people acquire the ideas, beliefs, values, and the like, of their society, and that these cultural features provide the basic materials by which they think and perceive.

Socio-cultural Space

Although cultural and social spaces have been separately discussed, they are in reality unified in one socio-cultural space. We do not live in one realm of culture and another of society. The two are not disjointed, but unified in a continuous whole within which meanings and values, cultures and super cultural systems, groups and individuals are located with respect to each other. Society and culture are but perspectives of the same phenomena. The components of this space, the common latent functions underlying the socio-cultural manifestations are located in this space.

Abstract Space

Abstract space is the space of logical relations that allow us to describe space without necessarily founding those descriptions in empirical observations. It is a free creation of the human imagination and as such is a direct reflection of achievement of symbolic thought. Kant presents an additional proof of his subjective space argument: "We can never represent to ourselves the absence of space, though we can quite well think it as empty of objects. It must therefore be regarded as the condition of the possibility of appearances, and not as a determination dependent upon them". Abstract space is also a term used in geography to refer to a hypothetical space characterized by complete homogeneity. When modeling activity or behaviour, it is a conceptual tool used to limit extraneous variables such as terrain.

Virtual Space

With proliferation of information technology virtual space is a virtual reality. It is a multi-user information space where users have a representation of their partners as well as themselves (Dieberger, 1999). This shared electronic environment constitutes of people involved in collaborative activities such as learning, working or playing in an environment that ranges from text-based interfaces to the most complex 3D graphical output. The key issue of this environment is that there is a spatial metaphor in which participants carry out a joint task. From the representation perspective, virtual environments are mostly more or less alike the physical world. Moreover, virtual environments integrate multiple tools so as to support different functions like information, communication, collaboration, learning, help and management. In this virtual space, communication tools, like text, audio and video channels are often used.

Narrative Space

Narrative space refers to the space that opens up in our lives when we realize that there are many new options and possibilities available to us based on various scenarios or stories that constitute our lives. It is never possible for one story to completely define any person, because as human beings we are more complicated than that. However it is often true that one story can be very influential in defining who we are. We call that the dominant story. For example, it is possible for someone to live out a story of him or herself as a failure, or a bad parent, or a drug addict. These stories can be equated with life position as described by Dr Eric Berne in "Games People Play."

Space In Astronomy

In astronomy space is referred collectively to the relatively empty parts of the universe. Any area outside the atmosphere of any planet or celestial body is generally considered as 'space'.

Philosophy on Space

An issue of philosophical debate amongst the philosophers is whether space is an ontological entity itself, or is it simply a conceptual framework. Since space appears as an enigma to human mind, philosophers in this ongoing debate frequently ask, "Can space itself be measured, or is space part of the measurement system?" The same debate applies also to time; which too is considered an aspect of space as per modern physics. A traditional pragmatic view is that time and space have existence apart from the human mind. Some however doubt the existence of objects independent of the mind. While on the other hand there are some whose ontological position is that objects outside the mind do exist, nevertheless they doubt the independent existence of time and space.

An important formulation in both areas of time and space was given by Immanuel Kant, in the 'Critique of Pure Reason'. He described space as an a priori notion that allows us (together with other a priori notions such as time) to comprehend sense experience. Kant, does not consider either space or time as substances, but rather considers both as elements of a systematic framework we use to structure our experiences. Spatial measurements are used to quantify how far apart objects are, and temporal measurements are used to quantify how far apart events occur. Similar philosophical questions concerning space include: Is space absolute or purely relational? Does space have any correct geometry or real dimensions, or is the geometry of space just a convention? Various positions in these debates have been taken by various scientists. Isaac Newton propounded that space is absolute; Gottfried Leibniz propounded that space is relational; while Henri Poincare mentioned that spatial geometry is a convention.

Mental Space

Robert M. Young, PhD a visiting professor at the Centre for Psychoanalytic Studies, University of Kent and a psychotherapist in his book 'Mental Space' writes about mental space as a contradiction in view of the mental and the spatial being defined *in* modern thought so as to be mutually exclusive. According to science, fundamentally, the spatio-temporal is thought to constitute nature. This leaves no reliable conceptual niche for the mental or the emotional. That is why 'mental space' is a problematic concept. Correspondingly a generic world view is; if something is mental, it can't be spatial, and if it's spatial, it can't be mental. Young further elaborates that the essence of the mental is thought; the essence of the spatial is shape or extension. How they relate is a profound and unresolved mystery at the heart of modern philosophy. He finally defines mental space as a space for reflection, for feeling, for relating to others, for being open to experience.

Gilles Fauconnier (1997) while describing the topology of mental space mentions that for purposes of local understanding and action mental spaces can be related to very partial assemblies constructed as we think and talk,. They contain elements and are structured by frames and cognitive models. Mental spaces are constructed and modified as thought and discourse unfolds and is connected to each other by various kinds of mappings, in particular identity and analogy mappings. Though mental spaces operate in working memory but they are also built up partly by activating structures available from long-term memory.Sigmund Freud while describing dreams located in the unconscious hinted at a spatial language which is not always based on physiological space but mental space represented in topographic patterns. (Robert M. Young, 1998). Further building up on this theory it can be reasonably assumed that everyone inhabits a mental space by virtue of thought. But our mental space is translated into 'reality' as a result of unprecedented communication means which we call the media. In mental space, communication and participation are key elements with script acting as the primary medium.

Strictly speaking, it is proven that the psychical systems are actually arranged in a spatial order and all psychical activity have a sense of direction and therefore are spatial. Psychical processes advance in general from the perceptual end to the motor end. The first point to be made about a different conception of mental space is the need for space itself. Robert M. Young, (1998) calls for sweeping away the baggage of scientist's Meta psychology. Meltzer justifies the existence of mental space in an account of 'Dimensionality as a Parameter of Mental Functioning.' According to him, insofar as an organism is concerned it has a mental life and does not merely exist in a system of neurophysiologic responses to the stimuli coming to it from internal and external sources. It lives in "the world" and this world may be variously structured. This four-dimensional world constitutes the "life space" of the organism. Meltzer further goes on to explain from the psycho-analytical viewpoint that this life-space may be said to comprise into four compartments inside the self; outside the self; inside internal objects; inside external objects; and to these may sometimes, perhaps always, be added the fifth compartment, the "nowhere" of the delusional system, outside the gravitational pull of good objects. These dimensions as per him reflect mental space of the individual, from conception to death. (Robert M. Young, 1998).

Theology on Space

In Upanishads Space has been mentioned as 'Akasa'. Defining space is not easy as it implies vastness and immensity. Space cannot be given any location as space itself is the very basis of the concept of location. 'Akasa' or space concept was used by vedantic thinkers as the best symbol of the Infinite and the Absolute, Brahman or Atman precisely because of its unlimited, ever pure, and indestructible characteristics. Swami Ranganathananda, (1993).

In Chandogya Upanishad there is a mention of a dialogue between three wise people on various aspects of spirituality. In one such instance, Salavatya asked Pravahana Jaivali about the goal of human existence. Prvahana Jaivali a knowledgeable soul replied that goal was Space, as all things originate from space; and they merge by moving towards space. According to him space was greater than everything and thus space was the supreme goal of life. He further clarified that space and Brahman were one and the same. (Swami Gambhirananda, 2000). Swami Shivarudra Balayogi popularly called Babaji by his devotees while addressing them in London in June 2005 spoke at length about space and Brahman and explained how space is God and vice a versa. He explained "Due to what we have been taught some feelings have been given about space, void, emptiness and such. That is why, if I say that this space is nothing but God, people may laugh. That is why you have to experience that this is not an inert void, it is Supreme Consciousness. Just like inside an earthenware pot the space is a Soul, but in reality the same Soul or Self is everywhere. The same Soul is within and outside also. That is what is meant when people talk about 'all pervading'. You also think, if it is all pervading, it has to be at every place. According to physics no two things can occupy the same space, so it has to be God. Space and God cannot be together in one place. Either it has to be the space and not God, or it has to be God. So that is how the Divine is all pervading. That is what it means that God and Space are one and the same." Similar views have been expressed by Swami Ranganathananda who mentions that it is very difficult to define space, as space implies vastness, immensity. Space cannot be given any kind of location. Space is here as well as there; it is inside as well as outside. In Vedantic language, therefore space or akasa is taken as the nearest symbol of the infinite and the absolute, Brahman or Atman. *"Puranamadah purnamidam purnat purnamudacyate; Purnasya purnamadaya purnamevavsiyate, Om santih, santih, santih-."* A sanskrit verse which precedes Isa Upanishad translates as " The invisible (Brahman) is the Full; the visible (world) too is Full. From the Full (Brahman), the Full (the visible universe) has come. The Full (Brahman) remains the same even after the Full (the visible universe) has come out of the Full (Brahman), describes the essence of space and God. Swami Ranganathananda, (1993). This verse supplements the views expressed by Indian sages over the ages that space and the Higher Self are one and the same.

Swami Nityaswarupananda (2004) further elaborates the above view while translating Astvakra Samhita. He mentions that literally, the space of intelligence is identical to Cit, Pure Intelligence. Cit has been conceived as akasa or space, because, like space, it is all pervasive and unaffected. Also all perception requires as an essential factor, the existence of akasa. Therefore three different akasa have been conceived : (1) mahaksa, the great space, which is the ordinary space in which we perceive external objects; (2) cittakasa, the mental space; everything that we imagine, dream, or supersensible perceive in the mental space; and (3) cidakasa, the intelligence space, the space in which the the Self perceives itself; here space is not something different from the perceiver and the perceived, as in the other two akasas, for in Self –perception it is all one, there is neither subject nor object; hence space is here identical with the higher

Self. Really speaking, in Self-perception there is no space; but the word ' space' is used to extend the analogy of the other two kinds of perception to Self- perception. (Swami Nityaswarupananda, 2004). Shankarachrya in Brahma-Sutra- Bhasya supplements these views by stating that space does not certainly originate and that (akasa) is Brahman, for a mark indicating Brahman is in evidence.(Swami Gambhirananda, 2000).

Space Time

Nature knows nothing of space and time separately. Time and space are integrated whole and not two distinct identities. (Swami Ranganathananda, 1993). The two are welded inseparably together into the product we may designate as "space –time". In physics, space and time are combined into a single construct called the space-time continuum. It is represented as a mathematical model. Space-time is usually interpreted as a four-dimensional object with space being three-dimensional and time playing the role of the 4th dimension. These views are substantiated by Euclidian theory, according to which our universe has three dimensions of space, and one dimension of time. By combining space and time into a single entity, physicists have significantly simplified a good deal of physical theory, as well as described in a more uniform way the workings of the universe.

Reichenbach a German scientist and philosopher who was a student of Einstein worked on the philosophy of relativity and was a critique of Kant. In his research findings he emphasizes the causal theory of space and time. According to him causality is the basis of both philosophical and physical theory of space and time. Causality plays a central role in Reichenbach's philosophy of science. Reichenbach uses the theory of causality as a key to provide access to modern physics and understanding of the philosophical significance of both the theory of relativity and quantum mechanics. According to Reichenbach, the causal theory of space and time is the basis for both the theory of relativity and the philosophy of space and time.

On the spiritual side while trying to identify what exactly are space, time and causation? The views of Swami Vivekananda who while trying to describe The Absolute as per Advaita (non duality) philosophy of Vedanta are of relevance. He mentions that The Absolute manifests itself as many through the veil of time, space and causation. He further goes on to elaborate that the combination of time, space and causation has neither existence nor non existence. (Swami Vivekananda, 1997). It is our human spectacles that divide them into space and time based on our perception. Due to our linear thinking it is the human mind that defines objects and events of the world of experience in terms of space and time continuum. Modern scientific thought however tells us that space and time have no absolute reality in themselves; they are relative concepts. It is only when they are welded together and become space time that they become a useful concept for the purposes of our modern day science. Therefore every event, in our world, is but a configuration of space-time. Thus it is this concept of space time that comes closest to our idea of that which is eternal, spiritual and infinite, in and beyond all finite entities and events. In fact time, space and causation are like the glass through which the Absolute is seen. As per Isa Upanishad it is inside everything, it is outside everything. It moves, and moves not. It is one and indivisible, but it appears to be divided by the passing events of the world of sense experience. (Swami Ranganathananda, 1993).

Other Views On Space

Leibniz saw space as being merely the relations between things; space as *per him* doesn't exist. Indeed in Leibniz's philosophy the absence of space, as well as the representation of that absence, is obligatory.

Norberg- Shulze mentions " pragmatic space integrates man with his nature 'Organic' environment, perceptual space is essential to his identity as a person, existential space makes him belong to social and cultural totality, cognitive space means he is able to think about space, and logical space offers him tool to describe the others." To these can be added space that integrates experience and thought.

Chapter 6

Life Space as it Manifests

On scrutiny of life and space separately it is quite evident that there is no single definition either of life or of space. Both entities are described by various knowledgeable people in different ways. Ordinarily we all understand the meaning of what is life and what is space yet their dimension is so huge that both entities cannot be confined to any one given definition. We must view life space as a single construct and not go by the two words that are its basic constituents. There is therefore a need to understand what life space is? Life space can be denoted as the sum total of all space relevant to humankind. It will encompass dimensions of physical, psychological, social, cultural, socio-cultural, narrative, virtual or abstract space that reflects the personality of an organism dealing with human beings. This organism can be an individual, group, society, organisation or nation. At the center of this space are our dynamic intentions, motives, attitudes, and sentiments; our super ordinate striving for self-growth, esteem and self-actualization; our phenomenal dependency and practical freedom. This dynamic space shades into defining our meanings and values, and our organized and semi-organized activities; also defining our cultural and socio-cultural systems. So life space as a single construct is space in its entire avatar in which human being exists individually or collectively. Similar views have been expressed by Nova Croft (2005) while describing intentional space. However life space encompasses intentional space as well.

Maier (2000) uses the term "life-space" in a more general sense to describe the whole social emotional, physical organizational and environmental context in which residential life takes place. According to him life space has three aspects, physical, social and organizational. This view of life space is very narrow in its dimensions as it is confined to residential life alone. This is restrictive and does not encompass all aspects of life space.

At the centre of life space is the human being who exists in his individual as well as collective capacity in this life space. Daniels while commenting on Kurt Lewin's field theory mentions that Kurt Lewin used the word life space describing it as the total environment of the individual and went on to conclude that an individual participates in many different life spaces such as family, church, work, or school. The behaviour of the individual was thus represented as movements through various life spaces that carry both positive and negative influences and are driven by individual's perceptions based on their underlying psychological needs. If we are to accomplish the task of deriving the behaviour of the person (in more general terms: the psychological events) from the life space, we have to characterize it as the "totality of possible events." Life space as a single construct integrates all forms and dimensions of space that influence and shape the existence and sustenance of the organism, be it physical, psychological, mental, virtual, abstract, narrative, intentional etc. The concept of life space is more abstract and has to be visualized as such. A diagrammatic representation is as given below:-

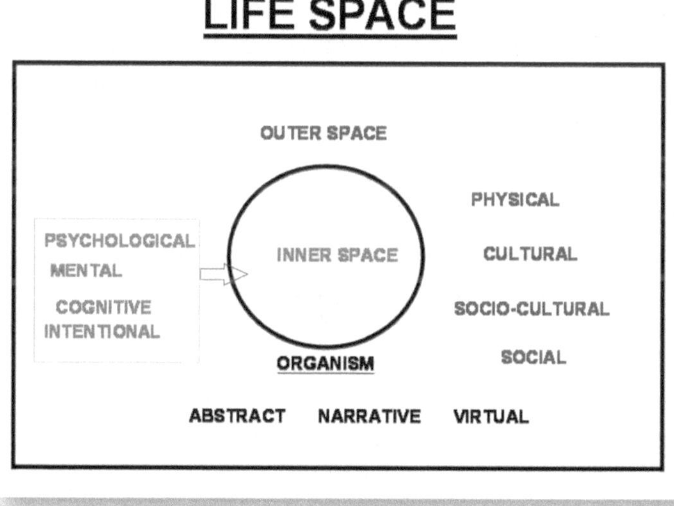

Figure 1 – Life Space.

The above diagram lists simply the components of life space. Moving from our inner world to our outer one, we have the outcome of this life space defining our actions and behaviour depicted by motivations, temperaments, abilities, and moods and states. In addition, we have the meanings and components of religion-philosophy, science, language, ethics-law and fine arts built into this whole construct. Then there are the status components of wealth, power, and prestige all influencing and shaping this life space. At the centre of all this is the organism who is radiating and trying to create its own space in the environment that is saturated with other organisms vying for the same space.

These views are substantiated by Lewin who defines life space as the totality of facts, which determines the behaviour of a person. He further states that this life space includes the person (P) and the environment (E). Behavior (B), according to Lewin is a direct function of the person and the environment B=f (P, E). Timothy Jordan writes that Lewin further goes on to elaborate that a person is comprised of two parts, the motor-perceptual and the inner-personal. The motor-perceptual region has the position of a boundary zone between the inner-personal regions and the environment. (Lewin, 1936).

Life space therefore emerges as an abstract concept/ phenomenon which encompass all dimensions of space in which an organism exists and functions. An organism creates life space to enhance its effectiveness in the environment that it operates and exists. Life space therefore emerges as a single construct signifying unity of all dimensions of space influencing an organism.

Life space depicts organic union of an organism with nature and its environment. This unity is bounded by an organism's dynamic psychological field encompassing perceptions, meanings, and values, social, biophysical and ecological relationship. Life space therefore generates a field that is dynamic in nature and influenced by motives, sentiments goals and actions. It gets its sense of direction also from the organism's intentions and the culture and society it exists in. This field is also deeply influenced by cognitive abilities and limitations of the organism. This field is finite but with flexible boundaries. Sometimes it expands and at times it shrinks. Even a single event can affect its zone of influence / boundaries for good or for bad depending on how it is perceived by the environment. RJ Rummel the author of "Understanding Conflict and War: The Dynamic

Psychological Field," has described intentional space and intentional field which supplements the views just expressed as both form an integral part of life space.. While Rummel has been concerned with the dynamic psychological field, with its tetrad structure, and especially with the manner in which intentions result in social behaviour; life space on the other hand is the total outcome of the intentions and subsequent behaviour. This is confirmed by Rummel when he explains that. "My purpose here has been only to describe the spatial framework of the intentional field and to suggest that the dynamic psychological field is only a localized field within a larger whole." Life space therefore is, in fact, one space, the space of an organism in its manifold dimensionality. This life space can be split up only for ease of understanding of the various constituents of life space.

Marking / Delineating of Lifespace

The physicist accept psychological facts as being non spatial in nature. An essential characteristic of this physical space is that it is thought of as a single coherent space which includes the totality of only all physical facts that exist at a certain time. The facts of psychology do not have visible physical dimensions and therefore according to the teaching of physics, they have no place within physical space. Nevertheless psychologists have been continually making efforts to coordinate dynamic facts in psychology to physical facts. Kurt Lewin too depicted life space in topological fashion. All representations of psychological life space he based on the fundamental conception of a particular person in a particular environment. Lewin worked out the details of the boundary between environment and person based on the conception of relationship and belongingness of the person to his environment. He attempted to determine mathematical existence and position of a certain boundary in the psychological life space in different ways according to the nature of the case under consideration. According to him it was possible to survey, for instance in the quasi-physical field, a number of regions simultaneously and determines the boundaries between them without difficulty. The determination of topological relationships is the fundamental task in all psychological problems. Changes of connection are the most important changes both in the psychological environment and in the structure of the person. Also the topological relationships are fundamental for the mathematical representation of psychological issues. These are based on the relationship between "part" and "whole" and on the concepts of "being included-in." Closely related to these is the concept of "surrounding" of a "point." While working out topology of life space Lewin assumed that space is infinitely divisible. It is possible to break up each region into part regions and therefore to distinguish part regions of part regions ad infinitum. This property of space he applied to life space to determine points in the life space in treating the psychologically unqualified regions.

Further elaborating on defining the fields of psychological representations Lewin draws a parallel between "phase space", and psychological space. In physics phase space is frequently used to represent a multitude of factors influencing an event. Phase space is different from the three dimensional physical space within which physical objects is moving. Lewin therefore confirms that in life space or psychological field in which psychological locomotion or structural changes take place cannot be equated with those diagrams where dimensions mean merely gradations of properties. (Kurt Lewin, 1959).

Life space is subject to behaviour and actions of an organism. Any behaviour or any other change in psychological field depends only upon the psychological field at that time. Within the realm of facts existing at a given time there are three areas in which changes generate interest in psychology as mentioned below:-

(a) **The Life Space.** The psychological environment as it exists for an organism. This field is generally considered while referring to needs, motivation, mood, goals, anxiety, ideals etc.

(b) **Processes.** A large number of processes undertaken in the physical or social world, which do not affect life space of the individual at that given time.

(c) **Boundary Zone of Life space**.   Certain aspects of physical and social world do influence and affect life space at that time. The process of perception for instance is intimately linked with this boundary zone; as also the execution of an action. (Kurt Lewin, 1959).

It is therefore quite evident that life space has defined boundaries which through psychological instruments can be predicted and defined. As per Lewin Life space can be divided into sub regions and the size of these sub regions can be predicted and measured and represented by geometrical or other mathematical means. He further elaborates that certain constructs in social psychology need to be refined. (Kurt Lewin, 1959). With this assumption it becomes evident that life space is finite in nature for anything that has boundaries is confined within the limits of that boundary. These boundary lines are not sacrosanct but are dynamic in nature that keeps changing with time and with change of any parameter of the environment. Due to its changing and dynamic nature in which life space keeps expanding and shrinking there is an urgent need to manage the change in life space so as to enhance rather than to retard the effectiveness of the organism under consideration. This needs an in depth study of Life Space Management as a concept for an understanding of its connotations and applications. This is more so in the contemporary era where pace of life has increased manifold, and different kinds of competing requirements are forcing individuals and organizations to adopt unfair means of creating life space for their survival. To create healthy living and existence both at individual and organizational level it is essential to understand and apply this concept. This phenomenon is true for all. Individuals and organizations must understand the rudimentary parameters that help in creating life space.

Chapter 7

Creation of Life Space at Individual Level

Every individual in this universe seeks his / her rightful place in the environment that it exists in. This rightful place differs from person to person based upon so many complex mechanisms involved in human behaviour, chief among them being cognitive ability, environmental influences, circumstances and karmas. This rightful place is created and sustained through life space management as also the entire effectiveness of an individual is an outcome of life space management. Human beings are the most complex species on earth. In order to understand individual effectiveness let us first understand the composition of the individual, for that will facilitate in defining and grouping the behavioural pattern of human beings.

The Indian scriptures analyzed man as having evolved from matter and matured to his present form through various stages of evolution. Indian scriptures have described them as five stages; generally known as 'Panch Kosh' or five sheaths. In the beginning matter evolved from the unmanifest to the manifest and was in existence for a very long time (Anmaya kosh, material s heath). Then creator put some vitality or pran into the matter (pranmaya kosh, vitality sheath). Then He added a mind to it (manomaya kosh, mental sheath). Then He gave knowledge (vijnanmaya kosh, knowledge sheath). The Divine gave knowledge to enter the state of supreme bliss from where the individual returns to the Creator. (anandmaya kosh, bliss sheath). The same has been amplified by Prof SK Chakarborty (1999) in his Yoga-Vedanta model of man as shown below :-

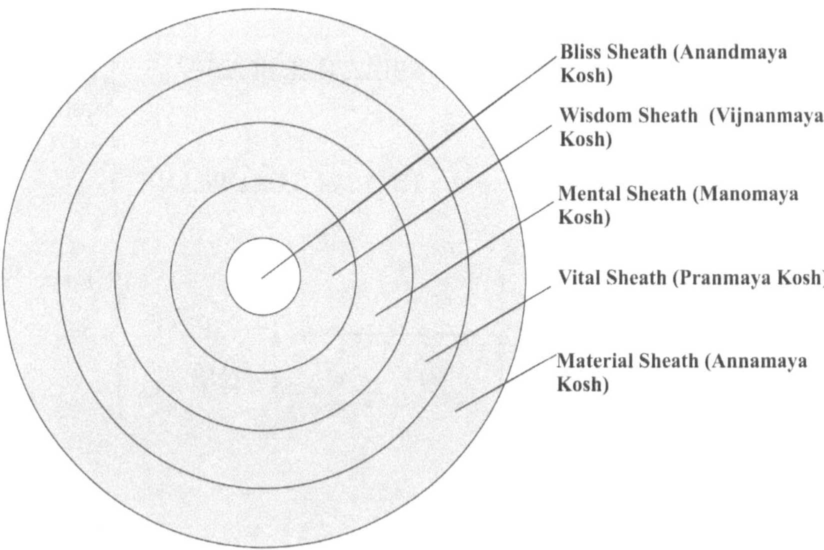

Figure 2 Panch Kosh Model

Prof SK Chakraborty (1999) goes on to explain that 'the three outer koshas or sheaths together could be treated as the equivalent of the Lower Self or little ego or prakriti, and the two inner most ones as constituting the Higher Self or real Self or Purusha. The professor further goes on to explain that since life evolved from matter, the material sheath is very large and powerful. Further analysis of Yoga Vedanta model of man reveals the evolution of human being to the highest plane of existence is a state of eternal bliss or Anandmaya kosh. The material, vital and mental sheath can be clubbed as physical plane of existence. The wisdom sheath as the intellectual plane of existence and the bliss sheath as the spiritual plane of existence as shown below:-

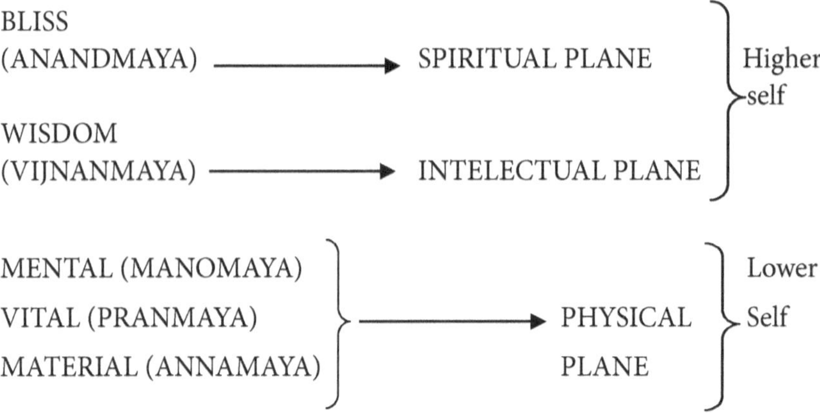

A human being has all these planes within him; but by and large a vast majority nearly 98% exists at the physical plane of existence. Approximately one to two percent exist at the intellectual plane of existence. One in million graduate to spiritual plane of existence. These figures are agues work and are not Those who exist at the spiritual plane of existence identify themselves with their real Self or the higher Self. Those who identify themselves with their lower Self; are people who lead a materialistic life; identify themselves with their physical bodies and worldliness: as Isa Upanishad describes that man at this stage functions at the animal level for mere sense enjoyment and experience. The world of objects comprises their sphere of awareness and of pleasure and pain. Life space management at the three planes of existence varies. The vast majority mired in maya,(illusion), lead a materialistic life.

Having identified the three planes of human existence; there is a need for in depth analyses of the application of life space management criteria and techniques at individual level with emphasis on its applicability to the vast majority who exist at the physical or materialistic plane of existence.

Human beings inadvertently resort to life space management without being aware of it. It comes naturally to human beings. Those who understand its basic parameters and practice them in their lives are more effective than those who do not observe them. From the analysis of the brain storming of the root criteria of life space creators at individual level; the order of precedence that emerges is as shown below:-

1. Love

2. Altruism

3. Communication

4. Character

5. Values

6. Personality

7. Respect

8. Positive attitude

9. Self control

10. Tact

11. Manipulation

The above parameters that create life space and how they need to be managed are studied in greater detail in subsequent chapters.

Chapter 8

Love

Love is a thread that binds people. Without love, life is like an empty pot. Love is an integral part of our existence. Every one craves to be loved. Children who are not loved are likely to suffer from Marasmus. Jesus Buddha, Prophet, Guru Nanank Dev, Lord Rama & Krishna are revered the world over because of the pure universal love that they gave. Even fiercest animals get subdued due to pure love. A living example is a Tiger Temple, or Wat Pha Luang Ta Bua, a Thervada Buddhist monastery in Thailand where the monks and wild tigers live in harmony with each other.

The Divine created the cosmos out of love. That is why all creations are born out of love. As the creation was born out of love it was filled with love. He created as part of a game to be played in which each creation has a role to play. The creator also made the game more interesting by creating opposites, a world of dualities. In this game of dualities He also created a devil which countered love by hatred. Human beings were endowed with both. Hatred led to the Ultimate Devil and Love to the Creator. The general belief is that the creator exists in all his creations. Like a painter exists in his paintings a musician of repute in his music similarly the Divine exists in all His creations. As the same creator exists in all; everything in this Universe is connected and related with the other. This relationship can only be comprehended when we start seeing and experiencing the Divine and his love in others. The thread that binds us or draws us together is love and that which breaks this bonding is hate.

Love is like scent, it permeates all boundaries. Pure love is bliss. Only through love do the lover and loved one become one.

Empedocles mentions that "love is invisible, a sacred and ineffable spirit which traverses the whole world with its rapid thoughts". In psychology there are several theories of love. In psychology love is depicted both as a cognitive and social phenomenon. Psychologist Robert Sternberg has propounded his triangular theory of love and argued that love has three different components: intimacy, commitment, and passion. Intimacy is a form by which two people can share secrets and various details of their personal lives. Intimacy is usually shown in friendships and romantic love affairs. Commitment, on the other hand, is the expectation that the relationship is going to last forever. Ericc Fromm, in his 'Art of Loving,' spells out his theory of love in which he mentions that every new born child wants to return to the secure environment of his mother's womb. This desire to return to his true nature is the basis of all love. Fromm states "every theory of love must begin with a theory of man, of human existence." He then goes on to describe man's anxiety arising from his separation from the rest of the universe and others in it, and love as a solution to that anxiety problem. This finding is supplemented by Dollard & Miller (1950) who mentions that love between mother (or caretaker) and child develops as she meets the primary needs and also provides thousands of positive reinforcements to the child. (Hewstone, Strobe & Stephenson, 1997).

Divine is an ocean of love. All his creations emerged from his heart filled with love. Thus all creations of the heart are born of love. Conception is thus the start point of all love. Mother falls in love with her unborn baby right from conception. It blooms and turns into intimacy, once the child is born and the mother gets to hold her child in her arms and snug the child to her bosom. Intimacy leads to bonding. Pure love leads to lifelong bonding. Greater is the bonding greater is the life space created.

Mostly at physical plane of existence we misconstrue lust as love. Lust is the physical desire for mating created by the divine for continuation of his creation. It is short lived and as per Helen Fisher lasts anything between 3 to 6 weeks. Another aspect of love at physical plane of existence is attraction which as per Helen Fisher too is short lived and lasts from one and a half years to three years. While pure love is eternal.

As per Plato 'Love is desire for the perpetual possession of the good.' (Lydia Amir, Nov 2001)

We love what is good and thus relevant to us. Relevance is also created by love. Hate diminishes and destroys relevance. Once decimated, the object of hate loses its relevance. Love on the other hand enhances relevance. Relevance leads to liking and liking to love. The cycle thus becomes complete. This is a two way cycle as shown below:-

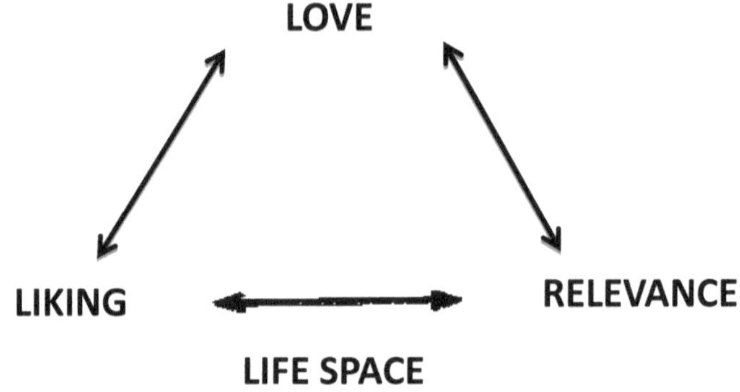

Figure 3 "Cycle of Love in Life Space"

With greater love infused the radius of the cycle increases. Greater is the radius greater is the life space created by love. Another aspect of pure love is that it is a value worth its weight in gold.

All religions of the world preach true love as practiced by various Masters. In Hinduism Bhakti Yoga or Bhakti Marg depicts the path to reach salvation through falling in love with the Divine. Bhakt becomes the lover of the Divine. As per Bhagwat Puran there are nine forms of true love that a Bhakta can pursue. Hinduism also speaks of Kama which is the sexual representation of love and its deity is Kamadeva with Rati as his wife. This is restrictive and does not lead an individual to the ultimate goal of liberation from the cycle of birth and death i.e. moksha. In Christianinty the New Testament speaks about 'agape,' which is described as charitable, selfless and unconditional love that creates goodness in the world. It is the way God is seen to love humanity and the Christians aspire to practice. In Islam Sufism is a projection of true love of the Divine. Sufism believes that through true love, humankind can get back to its inherent purity and grace. Parrels can be drawn between Bhakti Marg and Sufism. Buddhists believe in Karuna i.e. compassion and Maitree i.e. friendliness. Judaism preaches one to love God with all their heart, soul and might. It also teaches them to love their neighbor like themselves. (Internet   22/01/09)

Love is like space which is both within and outside. It is seamless and has no definite shape or size. The dimensions of love are defined by an individual. Lesser mortals confine their love to a very small circle of friends and relatives. While evolved souls radiate universal true love. True love is all about giving and seeking nothing in return. Great souls like Jesus, Buddha, Rama, Krishna, Prophet , Guru Nanak Dev all radiated true universal love and have thus got interlinked with a vast majority of populace. Though these souls died several hundreds of years ago their name itself creates a very large space with their followers. Such is the power and influence of true love. True or pure love emanates from a pure heart. Amongst the living relations mother universally creates the largest life space with us. This is because of the pure unselfish love she has for her children. This love of mother too is restrictive as it is confined to her own offspring only. If pure love is extended to the Universe the person becomes immortal like Jesus and Buddha.

Relevance of love is amply enunciated in an old Indian folklore. "Once upon a time an Indian sage was going along with his disciples to the banks of river Ganges for a bath, when he observed some members of a family shouting at each other. He very politely asked his disciples as to why the members were shouting and fighting with each other. The disciples told him that they were angry with each other. The sage further asked as to why people shout when they are angry. The disciples could not answer this question of the master. The sage then told them that anger is a manifestation of hate. It could be hatred of, word, act or person. Hate generates anger and anger distances hearts and therefore people have to shout to be heard. Love on the other hand reduces the distance between hearts and therefore people in love can understand each other even without uttering a word. He advised his disciples to reduce the distance of hearts through true love, for that is what a true yogi does."

Chapter 9

Altruism

Care is defined as anxiety or occasion for it, task, thing to be seen to, charge or protection, see to the safety, health, of, guard against losing; feel concern or interest. The word understand means to comprehend, perceive the meaning of, perceive the significance or explanation or cause or nature of, and know how to deal with. Understanding means, intelligence, intellect, insight; union of sentiments, convention, thing agreed upon, stipulation. Help means, aid assist, to serve; remedy, prevent, avoid. (Fowler & Fowler, 1961).These three words when considered together reflect a social character that is self sacrificing to help others with love care and understanding. The whole concept and underlying meaning in which the respondents have mentioned these words is the metaphor 'Altruism'; as it reflects regard for others as a principle of action.

There is a school of thought that believes that humans are pro-social and self sacrificing where altruism comes naturally to them. The other school believes that humans are hedonistic and resort to helping others with a motive. The motive could be social recognition that the helper is a good person. Schnieder (1976) defines altruism as behaviour for which rewards to another are important relative to self rewards. Altruism is not confined to humans alone. It is different that humans don't learn from nature. Evolutionary biologists use altruistic behaviour to refer to behaviour that that helps another individuals fitness despite a cost to the donor. Harcourt (19991) highlights that altruism prevails in the animal kingdom as well. Hewstone, Strobe, and Stephenson, (1997). Some examples of altruistic behaviour in animals is given below:-

   (a) A male olive baboon helps another male defeat a rival despite the risk of injury.

(b) A lioness will take care of other lioness cubs.

(c) There are tales of bitches feeding and bringing up cubs of big wild cats like tiger and vice versa.

(d) Tales of wolves bringing up human kids like Rudyard Kiplings Mowgli, and the legendary Romulus and Remus.

(e) In white ants soldier castes defend a termite colony with their lives.

(f) Wild dogs hunt co-operatively and share food with non hunters.(McFarland, 1993; Wilson, 1975)

Hamilton (1964) highlighted inclusive fitness to demonstrate altruistic or helping behaviour amongst the animals. Inclusive fitness emanates from the wider concept of fitness, when helping relatives is balanced against reproduction. When applied to humans, inclusive fitness explains why relationships are important in all human societies, why people help their close relatives. Kaufmann (1973) quotes (Reiss, 1962; and Susman, 1959) which too found that the closer the kinship, the greater the likelihood of mutual help.

Meyers (1993) mentions that altruism comes from social- exchange theory. He elaborates that human interactions are guided by "social economics." He quotes Foa & Foa (1975) that humans exchange not only material goods and money but also social goods i.e. love, services, information, and status; by employing minimax strategy. Minimise costs and maximize rewards. These rewards can be external and internal. This theory is contested as not all altruism is for selfish reasons of obtaining rewards. Michener, DeLamater, and Schwartz (1986) mention that there are three types of motivation to help. First, our values define that helping is the right thing to do. Second, people help in response to their own feelings of compassion or discomfort arising on seeing others in distress. Third, people help because they can obtain rewards or avoid costs. These three motives may work singly or in combination depending on the situation and which of them is more predominant at that stage.

People help others as an act of social responsibility also. In our society certain categories of persons are labeled as 'to be helped.' In India the scheduled castes and scheduled tribes are labeled as to be helped. People below the poverty lines are labeled as to be helped. Orphans and senior citizens are to be helped. Ladies in distress are to be helped. In olden days in India, this help was carried out as a matter of duty.

The word altruism is derived from French altruisme, probably from Italian altrui, someone else, and from Latin alter, other. Altruism is defined by various people as given in succeeding paragraphs:-

Jason Kreag a graduate student, Center on Philanthropy at Indiana University researched and wrote that the original use of the concept of "altruism" can be traced to Auguste Comte, a French mathematician and philosopher during the first half of the 18th century. The French word that was later translated to "altruism," was an adjective that meant, "of or to others, what is another's, somebody else." When the word was translated into English, it was defined as, "devotion to the welfare of others, regard for others, as a principle of action: opposed to egoism or selfishness." He further quotes Webster's Dictionary that defines altruism as, "consideration for other people without any thought of self as a principle of conduct." The injunction against any thought of self is what distinguishes the definition today.

Dr Roger Howells, FRC Psychology, private consultant psychiatrist, Chelsea, London describes altruism as unselfish concern for the welfare of others; or just selflessness. Andrew Reeve describes in greater detail as benefiting other persons. He further highlights the difference in selfishness and altruism, by differentiating in the disposition, intention, and behaviour. An altruistic person intends to benefit others, thus giving more consideration to others than oneself. In discussions based on game theory, he draws a contrast between reciprocal altruism and universal altruism. Reciprocal altruists display that behaviour towards those from whom they have received it, or from whom they expect to receive it. Universal altruism, often seen as the central ethical prescription of any religion, is unconditional. In socio-biological applications, it can be shown that the survival chances of individuals and groups depend not only on the incidence of selfishness and altruism, but also on the type of altruism in question.

Similarly Encarta dictionary defines altruism as **selflessness:** an attitude or way of behaving marked by unselfish concern for the welfare of others: **belief in acting for others' good:** the belief that acting for the benefit of others is right and good·

Relevance of Altruism in Various Fields.

Altruism impacts and influences several fields. Some these are listed below:-

Altruism in the Sciences

A number of studies have been performed documenting behavior that may be considered altruistic in the animal and insect world (Wilson, 1975; Darwin 1872). Developments in biology have allowed scientists to map the building blocks of life and to identify genes for specific traits. Several questions have been raised from time to time such as: is there a gene for altruism. Such a question has been the initial impetus behind George R. Price's development of the Price equation which is a mathematical equation used to study genetic evolution. An interesting example of altruism is found in the cellular slime moulds. These protists microorganisms live as individual amoebae until starved, at which point they aggregate and form a multicellular fruiting body in which some cells sacrifice themselves to promote the survival of other cells in the fruiting body. Social behavior and altruism share many similarities to the interactions between the many parts (cells, genes) of an organism, but are distinguished by the ability of each individual to reproduce indefinitely without an absolute requirement for its neighbours.

Altruism in politics

Based upon the political convictions, altruists may be divided in two broad groups: Those who believe altruism is a matter of personal choice (and therefore selfishness can and should be tolerated), and those who believe that altruism is a moral ideal which should be embraced, if possible, by all human beings. Lysander Spooner a political analyst, in Natural Law, writes: "Man, no doubt, owes many other moral duties to his fellow men; such as to feed the hungry, clothe the naked, shelter the homeless, care for the sick, protect the defenceless, assist the weak, and enlighten the ignorant. But these are simply moral duties, of which each man must be his own judge, in each particular case, as to whether, and how, and how far, he can, or will, perform them". Based on this natural law it can be said that altruism may take some form of collectivism or communalism too. It can therefore be stated that altruism is the kind of ethic that should guide the actions of politicians and other people in positions of power. Such people should set their own interests aside and serve the people. When they do not, they may be criticized as defaulting on what is believed to be an ethical obligation to place the interests of others above their own. In Indian context in the pre Independence era Indian politicians generally displayed political altruism and in post Independence era quite the reverse. The image of politicians today has taken a beating with the revelations of the number of scams that our politicians are involved in.

Altruism in History and Philanthropy

History is replete with examples of altruistic personalities who committed their entire life to the welfare and well being of others. History is thus full of biographies of such great people. In very recent times Mahatma Gandhi, Martin Luther King, Jr. Mother Teresa are some of the most popular names. Similarly, there have been several unknown to the world, true altruist who worked tirelessly as *nishkam karma yogis* for the well being of others and sought no publicity for their actions. Even today amongst our midst such philanthropic people continue to contribute their mite to the well being of humanity without seeking anything in return. The goal of philanthropic activity is to make things better for others. So far as this is true, the philanthropic sector can be described as a greenhouse in which altruistic activity is nurtured and cultivated.

Altruism and Religion

As altruism and morality are correlated all the world's religions promote altruism as a very important moral value. They all pay great emphasis on altruistic morality. Altruism was central to the teachings of Jesus as is found in the Gospel especially in the Sermon on the Mount and the Sermon on the Plain. Jesus preached love thy neighbour more than thyself. Hinduism teaches (*Nishkam Karam Yoga*) union through selfless action. In Srimad Bhagwadgita, Lord Krishna preaches Arjuna *Nishkam Karam Yoga*. He tells Arjuuna, " Your right is to work only, but never to the fruit thereof. Be not instrumental in making your actions bear fruit, nor let your attachment be to inaction." (Sloka 47, Ch2). He further preaches, "Therefore, go on efficiently doing your duty without attachment. Doing work without attachment man attains the Supreme. (Sloka 19, Ch 3). (Jaydayal Gondka, 1991). Guru Nanak too preached "Accursed are the lives and deeds of men who do not cherish the name of God. "(Prabhati,

1330) (Shan, 2002). . For Sikhs, altruism was made an act of faith by their founders. Guru Govind Singh Ji, the Tenth Guru of Sikhs, was at war with the Moghul rulers to protect the people of different faiths, when a fellow Sikh, Bhai Kanhayia, attended the troops of the enemy. He gave water to the injured, which revived their strength. It was under the tutelage of the Guru that Bhai Kanhaiya subsequently founded a volunteer corps for altruism. This volunteer corps till date is engaged in doing well to others and trains new volunteering recruits for doing the same. In love of altruism, there is no room for hatred or duality.

In Buddhism it is believed to be the best way to serve others and become a Buddha. Ven. Thubten Chodron (1993) elaborates and writes that the best way really to serve others is if we change our mind to one of altruism. By the force of having an altruistic intention and love and compassion, we take some effort to act constructively and so all of our constructive actions are pleasing to the Buddha and in time we become Buddha ourselves·

The concept of 'Itihar' a metaphor of altruism is practiced in Islam. The importance of itihar lies in sacrifice for the sake of the greater good. As per Islam those who practice īthār are the most noble human beings.

Altruism and Love

In philosophy, the problem of love questions whether the desire to do good for another is based solely on the outward ability to love another person because the lover sees something (or someone) worth loving, or if a little self interest is always present in the desire to do good for another. Love in its pure form is selfless. The French philosopher Pierre Rousselot (1878-1915) analyses this philosophical problem in terms of a pure "ecstatic" or totally selfless love versus an egoistic, more self-interested love. He analyses and examines Aristotle's writings *"Amicabilia quae sunt ad alterum vererunt amicabilibus quae sunt ad se ipsum";* Aristotle mentions that the friendly feelings that we bear for another arise from the friendly feelings that we bear for ourselves. (Alan Vincelette, 2001)

Relevance of Altruism in creating Life Space

Respondents while answering the factors that create life space with various people that they interact with, highlighted communication

,love, values care respect character , positive attitude ,understanding and self control/ self management as the top ten creators of life space. Care ,understanding and help when clubbed together under altruism highlights that altruism is a very dominant factor in creating life space with others. The details are listed in the tables given below:-

Total	
Factor	**Score**
communication	462
love/affection	301
values	255
care	**230**
respect	195
character	179
Positive attitude	126
understanding	**122**
self cont/mgt	110
help	**96**

Factor	**Score**
communication	462
Altruism	448
Love	301
values	255
respect	195
character	179
Positive attitude	126
self cont/mgt	110

Table 1 Factors of Altruism

Developing an altruistic behaviour

As altruism creates a huge life space the challenge is in developing an altruistic attitude. This can be developed by empathizing with others in the environment specially towards the needy. We must learn to accept people the way they are. There are a large number of living beings i.e humans and other living beings that need our help to sustain their existence. We must reach out to such living organisms with compassion and a desire to help from the heart without seeking anything in return. If someone seeks our help we must consider it as a God given opportunity to serve Him through that needy person or situation. Selfless altruism as preached in various religions and advocated by behavioural scientist must become an act of faith with individuals that must be practiced vigorously. Such altruist, *nishkam karma yogis* will create a long lasting positive life space with others in the environment.

Chapter 10

Communication

There can be no existence without communication. Every minute of our existence we are communicating. Even in sleep we communicate. Our body communicates how fast asleep or disturbed we are in our sleep. All our relationships with our environment are based on how and what we communicate. Even when alone, we communicate with our own self. So important is communication to our existence that some of us would die of depression if we did not communicate with the outside world. Communication therefore has been rated by the respondents as the most important factor in creating life space. Therefore let us understand the relevance of communication.

Communication is always with a purpose. When it is without a purpose it is glib and clutter. One of the purposes of communication is to bring about attitude or behavioural change. Roger D. Aprix (1996) substantiates these views and further mentions that while communication is an essential tool for bringing about change, it is often used poorly or thoughtlessly. Our quality of life is dependent on the quality of our communication with other people. Communication is also a medium of easing stress, conflict and psychological suffering. Wiemann & Giles (1997) quote Dance & Larson (1976) who mention that there are two characteristics which distinguish communication from behaviour. First for being able to code a message the sender of the message must be operating from some level of consciousness and with certain degree of intentionality. Second characteristic of communication is that it is an interpersonal process with dyad as the basic unit.

Our entire effectiveness in life is dependent on how well we communicate. Communication is intrinsic and is part of our existence since birth. An example of this is evident when on a lonely railway station if one has to wait for a train in the waiting room all by oneself on a lonely dark night. One longs for the company of another co-passenger. The minute another passenger enters the waiting room we non-verbally acknowledge the others presence with a smile or with a welcome gesture. This happens automatically without our being aware of it. Our interpersonal relations are directly related to the quality of our communication with the others. (Francis & Milbourn, Jr, (1980).

Communication has several meanings and working definitions. Physicists, mathematician, engineer, statistician or novelist, each give a different meaning to this term. To further understand the deeper meaning of communication let us understand how it has been defined by various people in the environment.

Leyton (1970) gives a generally acceptable definition that 'communication is transmitting a message in order to evoke a discriminating response'. The pocket Oxford Dictionary defines communication as " Imparting or exchange of information by message or otherwise, such message, common door or passage or road or rail or telegraph or other connection between places, connection between base & front." FG Fowler & HW Fowler(1961). Our concern is with the first definition i.e. exchange of information by message or otherwise. Similar views have been expressed by Pavaskar & Kulkarni (1978), according to them communication includes all methods of disseminating of information, knowledge, thoughts and beliefs. Caprara Cervone (2000) too mentions that communication includes more than linguistic exchanges. It involves multiple processes like social comparisons, imitation, symbolisation, paralinguistic expressions and other forms of non verbal emotional and behavioural expressions.

In philosophy dictionary http://www.answers.com/library/Philosophy Dictionary-cid-17265 communication is defined as the transmission of information; which emphasizes whether communication is essential to thoughts, or ideas, and what distinguishes a primitive signaling system, such as animals may possess, from full-fledged meaningful language.

Occultism & Parapsychology Encyclopedia deals with communication as the possibility of communication between the living and the world of the dead (spirits and nonhuman intelligences. Communication with the dead has been an integral part of human experience since the beginning of history. Communication from the dead may come in dreams. One of the oldest instances is given by Cicero in De Divinatione.

Wikipedia defines communication as a process that allows organisms to exchange information by several methods. Communication requires that all parties understand a common language and the medium of exchange. These medium could be auditory means, such as speaking, singing and sometimes tone of voice, or it could be nonverbal, physical means, such as body language, sign language, para language, touch, eye contact, or the use of written language.

Communication happens at many levels (even for one single action), in many different ways, and for most beings, as well as certain machines. Several, if not all, fields of study dedicate a portion of attention to communication, so when speaking about communication it is very important to be sure about what aspects of communication one is speaking about. Definitions of communication range widely, some recognizing that animals can communicate with each other as well as human beings, and some are narrower, only including human beings within the parameters.

Veterinary dictionary relates communication as that takes place between animals. This generally depends on sight and hearing and, on the sense of smell. The matters which animals communicate include recognition between mother and newborn; for mating; for initiating aggression or welcome; and for signaling danger or safety.

Relevance of Communication in Creating Life Space

There is a direct relationship between interpersonal relationship and life space. Good interpersonal relationship is the reflection of good and effective life space management. Poor relationship is an outcome of poor life space management. Life space is created by building rapport with the other person. To build rapport an individual has to pace his communications in such a way that it is fine tuned with the pace of the recipient. It is observed that active listening is a powerful tool for effective communication. There are various types of listeners. Anthony Alessandra(1986) identified four types; the non listener, marginal listener, evaluative and active listener. Non listener and marginal listeners hear but pay no attention to what is being said. Evaluative listener pays attention but does not understand the intent of the speaker. Active listener pays full attention to the content and intention behind the message. Carl Rogers popularized the term active listening and proposed five guidelines to perfect active listening.

(a) Listen to the content of the message by hearing precisely to what is being said.

(b) Listen to the feelings of the speaker.

(c) Respond to the feelings of the speaker by displaying and recognizing those feelings.

(d) Identify both verbal and non verbal cues of the message.

(e) Reflect back to the speaker what you are hearing by restating the message in your words that the speaker conveyed. This will help speaker to clarify and respond to the message.

Active listening is gainfully utilized by counsellors in building rapport and helping the individuals to find a solution to their problems. Active listener basically acts like a sounding board and everybody in this world wants to be listened to. Effective active listening becomes a very powerful communication tool to create sound life space.

Good and effective communication reduce time and space. It can also be said that time and spaces shrink due to good communications. Personal and economic growth is an outcome of good communication means and systems. Historically man has tried to explore and capture space and time in order to make progress; therefore his endeavour has always been to inject speed into his life. Wars have been primarily fought to satisfy this urge of humanity to control more space by encroaching on others space. This basic urge of speed is nowadays amply evident in the modern emerging communication technologies. Technically, all space/time restrictions have been effectively eliminated from the communicative process. We may now know everything as soon as it occurs and can say anything to anyone wherever they are. Clearly, we live in a global space and time continuum. We watch live coverage of events in real time on our TV sets. International events like world games, be they Olympics, football, cricket, tennis, or any other political event are now witnessed the world over in real time. In real time one can communicate with a near and dear one across the globe. News channels relay events in real or near real time. Location is no longer important so long as modern technology connectivity is available; with just a few clicks of a button (remote control, mouse, telephone) the world opens up. Communication technologies allow work to be distributed on a global scale. The British sociologist Giddens calls this as the differentiation of space and time. These modern communication means have revolutionized socialization. TV, internet and mobile phones have virtually become our social soul mates. The gurus of communication technology predict that faster processes will soon be available that ultimately would end the last barriers of space and time. Now knowledge is no longer a cultural product but now culture has become a communication or TV product. That is why those who watch a lot of television never have the impression that they are wasting their time. After all, they are communicating and that is supposed to be a cultural occupation. Today there is a conflict between the old and new generation ideologies. The old ideology supporters believe in returning to simple living of what can be controlled, to the space and time they are personally familiar with and are able to handle. Burgleman (2000). The new generation on the other hand lives more in a virtual world.

The credo of more, better, and hence faster communication has turned out to be a new ideology of technology and economic growth. The proliferation of information technology has been a great boon to Indian and global economy. Politicians now never stop stressing its necessity; managers consider it to be the panacea to almost everything. Management journals and books and newspapers are loaded with details with this topic. Human search to transcend time and space by use of modern communication technologies has generated an environment of surplus information. This in turn has resulted in the intellectual and social incapacity to deal with it. This further generates great amount of stress. People are increasingly looking for means to have some spare time as hither to fore, and thus overcome the rigours of stress full life they are now facing.

In short, people want to return from time to time to those moments in which time and space are irrelevant. This implies that while modern communication technologies may shrink physical time and space they do not influence or create life space. Life space being an abstract psychological space is not affected by technology. It is however deeply affected by inter and intra personal communications. In both these types of communication language plays a major role. Meaning can be given to any communication only through the medium of language. Language is a means by which we convey facts, ideas, attitudes and feelings to other people. Language may or may not be verbal. As professor Susan Stebbing has described in "Thinking to Some Purpose"; she mentions that language may vary from a simple mathematical language at one extremity to gesture language at the other. (Leyton, 1970). For creating life space what is the relevance of language. As language is the medium of communicating meaning to a message or text, appropriate language for creating life space is the language that achieves its purpose for what it is intended. This language must be the same as understood by the recipient. It should be simple and comprehendible. It should convey the correct meaning. It should not be ambiguous. The language should not be harsh abusive or threatening. It is said that language of the heart conveys true feeling and love. Language that conveys true love and not hatred will create largest space. This form of language is best witnessed between an infant and a mother. Communication with the purpose of creating life space will generate attraction through positive thoughts, feelings, attitude, and also through love and affection. Some of the practical methods of creating this life space are enumerated below:-

(a) **Verbal Communication.** One must communicate through a language that is well comprehended by the recipient. The communication must display respect, must be empathetic friendly and encouraging. Words must flow from the heart. We must not be too verbose and bore the recipient; on the contrary we should be good active listener and encourage the other person to talk and reveal about himself or his problems. Everyone wants to be heard and there are not too many people out there who want to listen to others. Humour breaks the tension and hence may be indulged from time to time. Only ensure that humour is not cheap and sarcastic.

(b) **Nonverbal Communication.** Non Verbal communication too must be in sync with verbal communication. Then communication becomes more meaningful. For creating meaningful life space our non verbal communication must display interest in the other person through use of proper body spacing and body language and other paralinguistic's.

People's identity, confidence in themselves and personal goals in life are strongly derived from interaction with others in the environment. From the beginning of life till its end an essential feature of human existence is the development of interpersonal relationships between the individual and others in the environment. These interpersonal relationships are rooted in quantum of life space created. The strength of the interpersonal relations is dependent on the capacity to Meta-communicate. Meta communication requires the knowledge of implicit rules of conversation and how they contribute to the maintenance of interpersonal relations. Mastery of communicative and meta communicative skills is essential for creating sound life space and harmonious interpersonal relationships. (Caprara & Cervone,2000).

Barriers to Good Communication

There are several barriers to good communication; chief among them being defects in human behaviour and personality. Any individual who operates from low self concept will always suffer from defective communication syndrome. The individual due to deficiencies in his personality will be defensive. Defensiveness is often a reflection of insecurity in individuals. It tends to distort perceptions as questions would be viewed as accusations and responses as justifications. There is a little wonder that effective communication often ends when the speaker or listener becomes defensive or offensive. In a self-perpetuating cycle of events, defensiveness/ aggressiveness, leads to more threats and accusations, and more defensive and offensive behaviours. These behaviours shrink and isolate the individual and thus reduce life space.

Improving Communication

Communication is an art that needs to be mastered. Why are film actors, TV person alities, preachers and politicians well known and popular? They all are popular as they have mastered the art of communicating. Bert Decker (2004) has identified nine behavioural skills required for effective communication. These skills are as given below:-

1. **Solid Eye Communication:** While talking look sincerely and steadily at the other person.

2. **Good Posture:** Stand tall and move naturally and with ease.

3. **Natural Gestures:** Be natural and relaxed while speaking.

4. **Appropriate Dress and Appearance:** Appropriate dress and etiquettes convey a lot of good and create a lasting impression.

5. **Voice and Vocal Variety:** Use voice as a rich resonant instrument.

6. **Effective use of Language and Pauses:** Use appropriate and clear language with planned pauses and no non words.

7. **Active listener involvement:** Maintain active interest of the people

you are communicating with.

8. **Effective Use of Humour:** Create human bond with the listener through good humour.

9. **Be your Natural Self:** To be authentic, just be your natural self.

Successful people channel their energy in creating a favourable environment through sound communication skills. All the great communicators have been observed to have a sound purpose of communication. Fundamental purpose of daily existence should be to personally feel and communicate happiness and love to others. Effective interpersonal communication begins with first understanding oneself through self communication. Only when one is able to understand personal strength and weaknesses that one is able to use them to ones advantage while communicating with others. (Hoogan, 2000). Sometimes it is better to seek external evaluation and help to improve our communication skills as it is often difficult to objectively assess how others perceive our communications style and the effectiveness. One very simple method of improving our communication skills is by observing and emulating persons who are excellent communicators. Some of the other methods are by getting external help in the form enumerated below:-

(a) **Mentor:** Seek a mentor and ask him or her to observe the way you communicate and then provide feedback and suggestions for improvements.

(b) **Seminars and Workshops:** These days there are several seminars and workshops being held at frequent intervals on improving personal communications.

(c) **Online Courses:** The present education system is not producing industry ready students. One of the major drawbacks observed is lack of communication skills. There are several entrepreneurs who are now offering online courses on enhancing communication skills.

(d) **Toastmasters:** Toastmasters is an organization which helps members improve their communications skills, particularly public speaking skills,. They also focus on improving presentation skills by providing constructive feedback. Join them and improve your communication skills.

Communication failures are costly. Communication failures can lead to conflict, loss of face, loss of business, loss of esteem and worth and above all loss of life space. It is therefore essential to focus on improving communication skills so as to enhance effectiveness in all aspects of our existence. Those who communicate appropriately well create a very large life space.

Chapter 11

Character

History is full of men of character. They left behind their legacy based on their good or bad character. Men of good character are revered while men of bad character are hated. Rama the legendary and mythological figure is revered as being a perfect human being with sound character while Ravan the demon king is despised and decried for his bad character. Parents of new born will name their son as Rama but no one names his son as Ravan. Ravan is a symbol of evil and Rama of virtue. In modern times, Mahatma Gandhi, Martin Luther King Jr, Mother Teresa, Nelson Mandela are remembered for their selfless service to humanity; all icons of good character.

What is of concern to our study is the nature of a personality. Quite distinct from the technical meaning which the term character possesses in logical sciences our focus is on the meaning attached to it in common life; as also in the literature devoted to psychology, values and ethics. The interest in study of character has been constantly increasing during the past hundred years. Character has been a source of great study and research and has been defined by various behavioural scientists in their own language. One such apt definition as given in internet (Apr 2008) is that character is a peculiar quality, or the sum of qualities, by which a person or a thing is distinguished from others. It is also mentioned in Mariam Webster Dictionary as the strength of mind; resolution; independence; individuality; as, he has a great deal of character. Thesaurus too defines character as the combination of emotional, intellectual, and moral qualities that distinguishes an individual. Character is also known by the physical qualities that describe a personality or moral or ethical strength of the personality and other distinctive element or traits of the personality. Encarta has also defined character as the set of qualities that make somebody or something distinctive, especially somebody's qualities of mind and feeling, typical or untypical of the behavior of a particular person or thing.

Actions reflect character of a person and these normally conform to the pattern the person has so far exhibited. A deviation is an indication of a more complex character than hitherto appeared. Character is the prime object of appraisal in virtue ethics and therefore actions are evaluated as good or bad, right or wrong.

Sports Science and Medicine looks at character as the personality structure or relatively fixed traits of an individual personality deemed culturally valuable or appropriate by society, for example determination and will to succeed. Sport is often said to develop character, but data supporting this assumption are sparse. Sachin Tendulkar and Vinod Kambli are contemporary cricketers with diverse character.

Psychology and Character

In lay mans language character is thus described as the expression of human personality. Only human beings and not animals have character. In general usage, the term is also employed in a narrower sense, as when we speak of a man "of character". In this connotation character implies a certain unity of qualities with a recognizable degree of constancy or fixity in mode of action. It is the subject of psychology that analyses the constituent elements of character and also traces the chief agencies which contribute to the formation of different types of character, and to classify such types. French psychologists have done intense research on the topic of character. Chief amongst them have been: MM. Azam, Pérez, Ribot, Paulhan, Fouillée, and Malapert. Still there is so much more to be researched as these contributions are not found to be adequate to summarise the subject.

Some of the behavioural scientists have stated that certain qualities of character could be inherited and the others acquired. The behaviour of each human being in any given situation is the outcome of a complex collection of elements. Resultant behaviour is dependent on perception and the thoughts and feelings that are generated by it; and the willingness that emanates and is peculiar to the individual, in spite of the common environment in which he participates with other human beings. Taken collectively they are said to constitute and reveal his true character.

Psychoanalysis: Character

Sigmund Freud dwelt with the concept of character in "The Interpretation of Dreams" (1900). The role of fixations emerged more clearly in 1905 In Three Essays on the Theory of Sexuality. Freud in 1905, emphasized the role of sublimation in character formation; He then described various character types associated with the partial drives in "Character and Anal Eroticism" (1908). Even Indian yogis have prescribed sublimation of sexual energy for attaining nirvana. In 1923, with the introduction of the structural theory, character was observed to be located in the ego which makes an essential contribution towards building up of character. Freud also observed that there was a degree of overlap between character and symptom. He further elaborated that despite their differences it was the failure of the defensive function of character that led to repression and neurosis.

Jean Bergeret (1976) described character as a power from the deep structure in relational life. He noted that elements of the fundamental character are often associated with elements of other forms of character, compensating for deficiencies in fundamental character through adaptive requirements. He further observed that character pathology corresponds to the "borderline" economy and its decomposition leads to a deformation of the ego.

Character and Reputation

There is a strong connection between character and reputation. Good character leads to good reputation and bad character to bad reputation. From the above statement it is evident that character can be classified into good or bad. In reality various classifications of types of character have been adopted by different writers. Some have classified character as the intellectual, the emotional, and the volitional or energetic. While some have classified it as lively, slow, ardent, and well-balanced. M. Ribot classifies character as humble, contemplative and emotional. He further classifies it based on energy levels as the active, subdivided into the great and the mediocre; and the apathetic, subdivided into the purely apathetic or dull. By combination these again afford new types of classification. M. Fouillée takes sensitive, intellectual, and volitional for his scheme and by cross-combinations and subdivisions works out an equally complex classification. Character can thus be objectively judged; it can be defined as right or wrong, good or bad. Good character traits include honesty, trust, respect, responsibility, leadership, loyalty and courage etc. And while character traits are universal, each individual has the choice to accept or reject them. Father Knuckles (2004) describes character as what a person is; and reputation to what he is supposed to be. He further elaborates that character is intrinsic to the individual; reputation is a picture in the minds of others. Character is harmed by temptations, and by wrongdoing; reputation by slanders, and libels. Character endures throughout defamation in every form, but perishes when there is a voluntary transgression; reputation may last through numerous transgressions, but may be destroyed by a single, and even an unfounded, accusation or aspersion.

Character and Correlation

From the surveyed results character is found to have a positive correlation with values. This confirms the observation of Father Knuckles. Sound values lead to sound and healthy character and negative values lead to a negative character. When correlation of character is analysed in reference to the various personalities, it emerges that it has a positive correlation with soldier, parents and teacher in that order and negative with a politician. In modern day in India, people associate a soldier, parent and teacher as possessing sound positive values and a politician with negative values. Positive values are also related to positive thoughts and positive attitude. James O. Pawelski is Assistant Professor of Human and Organizational Development and Religious Studies at Vanderbilt University, has done research on positive psychology for assessment of character. Positive psychology is a new and rapidly expanding field focused on the empirical study of human development. One of its central missions is the development of an operationalised classification of the strengths and virtues that constitute character. Positive psychology was launched in 1998 by Martin Seligman during his term as president of the American Psychological Association, so it is a new field of psychology. One of the functions of positive psychology is to identify the core virtues that are consistently valued across cultures and across time. The main virtues identified are wisdom, courage, humanity, justice, temperance, and transcendence. For positive psychology, good character is a function of these six virtues. In order to facilitate the definition, cultivation, and measurement of character, positive psychologists have ranged a total of twenty-four strengths under the six virtues. (Seligman, Martin EP, 2002)

They are as follows:-

Wisdom and Knowledge

1. Curiosity/ Interest in the World.

2. Love of Learning

3. Judgment / Critical Thinking /Open-Mindedness.

4. Ingenuity/Originality/Practical Intelligence/Street Smarts

5. Social Intelligence/Personal Intelligence/Emotional Intelligence.

6. Perspective

Courage

7. Valour and Bravery.

8. Perseverance/Industry/Diligence.

9. Integrity/Genuineness/Honesty.

Humanity and Love

10. Kindness and Generosity.

11. Loving and Allowing Oneself to Be Loved

Justice

12. Citizenship/Duty/Teamwork/Loyalty

13. Fairness and Equity

14. Leadership.

Temperance

15. Self-Control.

16. Prudence/Discretion/Caution.

17. Humility and Modesty.

Transcendence

18. Appreciation of Beauty and Excellence.

19. Gratitude.

20. Hope/Optimism/Future-Mindedness.

21. Spirituality/Sense of Purpose/Faith/Religiousness.

22. Forgiveness and Mercy.

23. Playfulness and Humor.

24. Zest/Passion/Enthusiasm.

Character and Life Space management

Who creates larger space, a person with good or bad character? Normal human beings would agree that a person with good and virtuous character creates a larger space. Strong and virtuous character creates further larger space. Respondents felt that character can effectively create up to 45.06 % of life space with them. It is therefore that character has been rated as a large creator of life space. Good character comes from good values. Good values generate good and positive thoughts. Positive thoughts over a period of time develop into positive beliefs and attitudes. So normally a strong and virtuous character will also have healthy and positive attitude. He will operate from his higher self. He will be spiritual in nature. He will trust in his abilities. (Peale, 1997).He further elaborates that individual will seek happiness in every situation, and will not dissipate his energies in fuming and fretting but will seek delight in the achievements and progress of others.

A man of character normally being spiritual the focus is internal as compared to external. Also the locus of control of such a person is internal. As Rabindranath Tagore mentions that Europe's socialites waste their time and energy on the external like hunting, dancing, dining, playing games etc. He advises humans to make acquaintance with the secret hermitage of the inner self. Only then can life save itself from wastage. He further elaborates that our original refuge lies within. This has to be felt repeatedly in the midst of all our activities. This inner chamber is always keeping and fencing around a free space in the midst of our crowded, noisy field of work. That free space is not mere emptiness. It is brimful with affection, love, joy and goodness. (Chakraborty & Bhattacharya, 1999). When we become aware of the inner self we radiate a sound character that creates immeasurable life space with others. Character can be developed by self effort, perseverance and sincerity.

Chapter 12

Values

Values as a subject have captured the interest of researchers, practitioners, social critics, and the public at large. These days every organization is busy spelling out the values they cherish and what values the organizations want their employees to have. Despite this attention, there continues to be a conspicuous lack of agreement on what values are and how they influence individuals. Meglino and Ravlin (Apr 2008) describe values as desirable modes of behaviour. Edward de Bono (2005) the leading authority on creative thinking, mentions that values influence all areas of thinking and behaviour. He further elaborates that values are considered important but not necessarily people are conscious of them. Morality is a social concept in which values play an important role in social interaction and behaviour. Jennifer (1987) describes that all humans have moral values and all make their own moral judgments. She further writes that the desire to act in accordance with ones values can transcend the desire for survival. So strong can be the impact of values.

All religions of the world preach existence by following moral values. Christian theologians suggest that human beings must contemplate on the picture of God in heaven and achieve the same through Grace. Grace can be achieved through a virtuous existence. Greek philosophy also emphasizes on virtue as an essential part of full life and self fulfillment. Similarly Indian Vedantic philosophy recommends human beings must aspire to become 'Poornatva' surplus inspired higher self. They must rise above the deficit driven lower self. (SK Chakraborty, 1999). Swami Vivekananda mentions that the goal of all nature is freedom and freedom is to be attained by perfect unselfishness that takes us towards the goal of freedom and as such is called moral. (Swami Mumukshananda, 1998). While western literature focuses on external dimensions and values that affect this form of existence, Indian scriptures focus on the inner core of human construct. Rabindranath Tagore too voices similar concerns. In his writings it is revealed that the poignant psychological crisis that consumes humanity arises from unrecognized disposition to locate and fix existential achievements in the external milieu. The real '*tirath*' pilgrimage spot lies within and can only be visited by contemplation and sound moral values that purify the inner core. (Chakraborty & Bhattacharya, 1999).

Man is an integral part of the whole; this is the basic Indian philosophy. Even Adler had similar views that a human being is a unified and self consistent organism. (Hjelle & Ziegler,1992). This philosophy is not well comprehended by vast majority. All humans have to co-exist with others in family, group, society or organizations, nations and this world. For mutual sustenance and benefit individual self interest must be sublimated and integrated with collective interest and wellbeing. Values harness this energy for collective and individual well being. (Swami Yuktananada, 2003).

Types of Values

Values can be classified as individual or personal values, family values, group values, team values, organizational values, cultural values and national values. The classification is dependent upon the location fixed for evaluation and classification. Managerial literature claims that values originate from vision. Human values vary from culture to culture. Chakraborty (1999) sees congruence between culture and human values. He observes three aspects of this phenomenon as given below:-

(a) Universal, trans-cultural human values as ideals.

(b) Culture specific, operative human values that translate into actionable conduct in a given culture.

(c) Culture specific, human values that derive from certain different human ideals.

Results of Survey

From the study it emerges that values can effectively create up to 41.06% life space with the respondents; which is substantial. It also emerges to have a positive correlation with character. Amongst the personalities it is observed to have a positive correlation with parents, intellectuals/ teachers, soldiers and friends in that order. It has a negative correlation with super rich, king/ queen and politician in that order. These observations reveal and supplement the belief that character and values go hand in hand. In Indian society parents, teacher, soldier and friends are revered for their positive and good values. The super rich and power brokers like heads of government and politicians are believed to possess negative values. From this analysis it is evident that perceptually maximum life space is created by parents followed by intellectuals/ teachers, soldiers and friends in Indian society; while the super rich and politicians create negative life space due to their disposition to disvalues. This analysis is generic in nature and will change from individual's disposition towards values or disvalues.

Relevance to Life Space

Sound values create a sound life space. Values have a very strong and positive correlation with character. Good and positive character is formed by good and positive values. In positive psychology, good character is determined as a function of six core virtues that are consistently valued across cultures and across time. The main virtues identified are wisdom, courage, humanity, justice, temperance, and transcendence. In all our decision making values play a major role. Values affect our thinking, perceptions and actions. Values are the drivers of emotions. Bono (2005). Traditionally the word value is viewed as having a positive impact. Negative impacting values can be labeled as disvalues. Disvalues generate negative thoughts, words and attitude and thus bring up negative and unhappy moods and actions. Disvalues thus poison human existence and environment; which causes more unhappiness and negativity. This is certain way to failure, frustration and disappointment. Disvalues like all negative things do not create life space, on the contrary they reduce life space.

Chapter 13

Positive Attitude

Attitudes determine the state of worldly human existence. It is the foundation for every success and every failure. Attitudes make or break an individual; therefore great relevance has been given by the respondents of the surveyed sample to positive attitude. Attitudes lie somewhere between our emotions and our thoughts and reflect our emotional perceptions about life, about others and even towards our own selves. Attitude generates feelings about people and situations. Individual actions are a result of their attitude, which, in turn, creates a reaction from others. It is our attitude toward others that determines the resultant attitude toward us. Attitudes generally express positively and negatively. A positive, joyful attitude generates positive, joyful results and negative attitude, the reverse. Human Resource personnel pay great emphasis to attitude while selecting people for their organizations.

Definition of Attitude

Attitude has been defined by various authors differently. An unknown author defines attitude as the way people mentally look at the world around them and the focus they develop towards life itself. Harry Kaufmann (1973) quotes Allport (1968) who defines attitude as " A mental and neural state of readiness, organized through experience, exerting a directive or dynamic influence upon the individuals response." Robert A Baron & Donn Byrne (, Jan 1998) in Social Psychology quote Fazio & Roskos Ewoldsen (1994) to define attitude as associations between attitude objects of the social world and evaluations of those objects . They further go on to describe that these evaluations are stored in memory and can be recalled at will (Judd et al., 1991). Similar views are also held by Gibson Ivancevich and Donnelley (1979). They state that 'attitude is a mental state of readiness, organized through experience, exerting a specific influence upon a person's response to people, objects and situations with which it is related.' Zimbardo, Ebbesen, and Maslach(1997) too concur with these views and mention that attitudes consist of satisfactions and dissatisfactions for attitudinal objects. They further elaborate that attitudes are regarded either as mental readiness or implicit predisposition that exert some general and consistent influence on a fairly large class of evaluative responses. Attitude can also be defined as organisation of several beliefs around a specific social world object or a situation. VSP Rao & PS Narayan (2000) define attitude as predisposition of the individual to evaluate some object in a favourable or an unfavourable manner.

It can also be said that attitude is a complex mental state involving beliefs and feelings and values and dispositions to act in certain ways. Further Wikipedia, the free encyclopedia defines attitude as a hypothetical construct that represents an individual's like or dislike for an item. Attitudes are thus positive, negative or neutral views of an "attitude object": i.e. a person, behaviour or event. Jung(1921) defines attitude as a state of readiness of the psyche to act or react in a certain way. Attitudes represent a more or less permanently enduring state of readiness of mental organization which predisposes an individual to react in a characteristic way (Cantril, 1934).Thurstone, (1931), defined attitude very simplistically as the affect for or against a psychological object. Similarly Bem, (1970) mentioned that attitudes are likes and dislikes. A recent definition given by Eagly & Chaiken, (1993) is in consonance with what has emerged earlier. They define attitude as a psychological tendency that is expressed by evaluating a particular attitude object with some degree of favour or disfavour.

Components of an Attitude

VSP Rao & PS Narayan (2000), mention that attitude comprise of three vital components – affective, cognitive and overt. Similar views have been expressed by David J Schneider (1976), he emphasizes on the cognitive, affective and behavioural component of the attitudes. This view is further supplemented by Harry Kaufmann (1973) while dealing with the formation and organization of attitudes. Affective component refers to the feeling or emotions that an individual has towards an attitude object. It is generally expressed on a continuum of dualities as good or bad, pleasing or displeasing, favourable or unfavourable etc. Osgod and Tannenbaums (1955) have based their congruity formulations which predict attitudes or cognitions solely from their polarization on the single affective dimension. Cognitive component represents the beliefs of a person about an attitude object. It is expressed as an opinion such as good / bad, favourable/ unfavourable etc. Rokeach (1968) asserts that the acceptance of a belief or sub system of beliefs is directly proportional to its degree of congruence with our own belief system. The overt component also known as behavioural or conative component reflects the tendency to react towards an attitude object in a specified way. VSP Rao & PS Narayan (2000). Andrew Michener, John D. DeLamater & Shalom H. Schwartz (1986) too supplement these observations and suggest that attitudes have three component; (1) beliefs or cognitions; (2) a favourable or unfavourable evaluation; and (3) a behavioural disposition. Harry Kaufmann (1973) quotes Sherif, Sherif and Nebergall (1965) who mention that attitude can be understood only in terms of a continuum of positions. Attitudes can also be differentiated in terms of their valence, multiplexity, relation to needs and centrality. Valence defines the degree of favourableness or unfavourableness towards the attitude object or event. Multiplexity defines the number of elements constituting the attitude. Relation to needs gives out the need that an attitude serves at a particular time. Centrality gives out the importance of the attitude object to the individual. VSP Rao & PS Narayan (2000).

Attitude Formation

It can therefore be inferred that attitudes strongly influence our social thought and resultant social behaviour. Robert A Baron & Donn Byrne (1998). Social psychologists agree that other than a few genetically acquired attitudes the vast majority are learned either through the process of social learning or through classical conditioning i.e. Learning based on associations. Andrew Michener, John D. DeLamater, Shalom H. Schwartz (1986) describe attitude formation as a process of reinforcement of stimuli i.e. instrumental learning, through association of stimuli and responses (classical conditioning) and by observational learning. Only a small portion of our attitudes are based on direct contact. VSP Rao & PS Narayan (2000) too feel that people are not born with specific attitudes but acquire them from the environment through the process of learning. Attitudes are thus acquired from family, society, peer groups, other group associations and experience by direct contact with an attitude object, There is a mutual reciprocate relationship between attitude and behaviour; both generate and influence each other like chicken and egg. (David G Meyers, 1993).

Attitudes and Behaviour

Do attitudes influence behaviour. The general public concept and view is yes. However social psychologists differ. Fazio & Roskos Ewoldsen (1994) recommend that moderators influence the extent to which attitudes affect behaviour. These moderators generally are certain aspects of situation, attitudes and individuals. Even cognitive theorists and reinforcement theorists differ in their views about the relationship between attitudes and behaviour. VSP Rao & PS Narayan (2000). The most famous research work on the relationship between attitudes and behaviour has been done by Richard La Piere between 1930-32.. Behaviour is directly influenced by the strength of the attitude. Attitudes acquired on the basis of direct experience exert stronger influence than those formed indirectly through hearsay etc. Attitudes that are acquired through direct experience are easy to bring to mind and thus greatly impact on behaviour. Robert A Baron & Donn Byrne (1998). Attitude strength, attitude accessibility and attitude specificity deeply influence behaviour. Petkova, Ajzen & Driver (1995) highlight; that strength of an attitude reflects the intensity of the attitude, its importance, knowledge and accessibility. Intensity depicts the strength of the emotional reaction provoked by the attitude object. Krosnick (1988), highlights attitude importance as the extent to which an individual cares for the attitude. It also reflects in addition to self interest and social identification the values of the individual. Knowledge implies how much the individual has knowledge of the attitude object. Attitude accessibility reflects the strength of the attitude object evaluation and memory link. The ease with which attitude can be recalled by memory. Attitude specificity reflects the extent to which attitudes are focused on specific objects or situations. Robert A Baron & Donn Byrne (1998). It is not only the attitude that influences behaviour, the reverse too is true. Many streams converge on this theory. Three theories are very popular and explain why our actions affect our attitude. Self – preservation theory assumes that people who desire to create a good impression normally self monitor their behaviour and adapt their attitude to appear consistent with their actions. Dissonance theory highlights that decisions produce dissonance. The change in attitude is brought about because people feel tension acting contrary to their attitudes. In order to reduce this arousal of uneasiness individuals internally justify their actions and behaviour. The more is the dissonance, more is the attitudinal change. Self- perception theory (proposed by Daryl Bem, 1972) assumes that when attitudes are weak individuals infer their attitudes by observing and analyzing their behaviour and circumstances. (David G. Meyers, 1993)

An Internet site (lucymacdonald.typepad.com, Mar 2008) quotes Khalil Gibran as "Your living is determined not so much by what life brings to you as by the attitude you bring to life; not so much by what happens to you as by the way your mind looks at what happens". Further Funmi Wale – Adegbite mentions that success is 80% attitude and 20 % aptitude. An unknown author has mentioned that "Your attitudes and the choices you make today will be your life tomorrow, build it wisely." Napoleon Hill supplements these views "Your mental attitude is something you can control outright and you must use self-discipline until you create a Positive Mental Attitude -- your mental attitude attracts to you everything that makes you what you are."

Attitudes being organisation of beliefs are never seen directly. Their existence is inferred from what people do. They include positive and negative evaluations, emotional feelings and certain positive/negative tendencies in relation to objects, people and events.

Mental Attitude

Mental attitude is the outcome of thoughts and beliefs. Thought is causal and creative, and appears in character and life in the form of results. Condition of life depends upon the dominant mental attitude at that given time. This could either be positive or negative. Limitations of one's nature are an outcome of one's thoughts. While ancient Indian scriptures define human being as infinite in nature. Practically human beings create self erected mental boundries the dimensions of which vary from person to person. Negative thoughts generate negative attitudes which in turn express the limitations of human nature and behaviour. Positive thoughts on the other hand demolish these limitations and present human nature in its pure infinite form.

Negative Attitude

Negative attitude is an outcome of negative thoughts. These negative thoughts generate negative beliefs. These negative thoughts and beliefs generate negative emotions. Over a period of time, this latent accumulation of suppressed negative emotions in human psyche develops negative attitude towards life; thus manifesting as a weak personality with low self concept. Such individuals appear to be apathetic, lost the battle of life and resigned to their fate. They draw their boundaries, enter their cocoons and feel comfortable there. Frustration, uncontrolled anger, bitterness, excessive shame, guilt, arrogance, envy, jealousy, greed, fear, suspicious nature, inferiority complex, persistent agony or melancholy, mental instability, escapism or dilly-dallying tendencies, communication apprehension, poor will power, low grasping, absentmindedness, sloth, laziness, dawdling, dodging etc are the outcome of negative attitude. Normally people facing such adversities tend to blame others or even to their own fate for their failures. Obviously they could not tolerate the grace, success or progress of others. They get resentful and bitter when they find that others are happy. Their surrounding factors can bring only the resentment and ultimately frustration for them.

Negative thoughts, words and attitude bring up negative and unhappy moods and actions. When the mind is negative, poisons are released into the blood, which cause more unhappiness and negativity. This is the way to failure, frustration and disappointment and ill health.

Aggressive Behaviour

People with negative attitude manifest an aggressive or passive behaviour. To cover up their deficiencies they adopt aggressive behaviour specially when under pressure. Such personalities with low self concept respond with explosive anger to a difficult situation. To cover up their weakness such people resort to unwanted shouting, swearing, using intimidating body language like thumping or pointing fingers, invading some ones personal space etc. Such actions are amply evident on Indian news channels where political opponents shout each other out specially during the election period. Such people want to win an encounter at all costs by refusing to listen, interrupting, shouting down or by undermining and upsetting the other person. Such manifestations of negative behaviour, results in loss of respect and life space. Also several normal people suffer from sense of guilt and shame and frustration after their outburst. Physically, such aggressive behaviour reflects signs of stress like rapid breathing and increased pulse rate, loss of concentration and logic. (Paddy O' Brien, 1992).

Passive Behaviour

Several people with negative attitude display a passive behaviour, wherein they give up responsibility for themselves and their actions. They feel that the whole world is against them. Such people display lack of energy and ideas, depressive body language, seek self pity, display martyr's attitude, use special pleading, and demand extra time and support.

Impact of Negative Behaviour

The impact of such negative attitude and resultant behaviour on personnel at the receiving end is also not healthy. People when subjected to such aggressive behaviour feel threatened equally angry or outraged, resentful, frustrated, hurt, resistant, vengeful or just confused. When subjected to passive behaviour they feel demotivated, let down, bored, lack of energy, restless and loss of confidence.(Paddy O' Brien, 1992). As per Carl Jung's introversion- extroversion schema theory of personality a negative attitude person is introvert in nature. An introvert is less sociable; normally withdrawn, recluse, rigid, guided by own ideas and philosophy of life. VSP Rao and PS Narayana (1987).

Chuck Gallozzi labels negative thinking as an insidious disease known as 'negativitis'. As per him it is as common as the common cold, but far more damaging. It debilitates and corrodes the human spirit. Those infected by it are broken men and women who aimlessly brood and become either confrontational or apathetic or just plain cynical. He further compares their lives to flat champagne, without any fizz. He further labels a negative attitude as a rotten attitude; that not only delays success, but also shortens life by damaging the immune system. In addition to the diseases directly caused by stress, such as heart disease and ulcers, individuals become susceptible to all manner of other diseases because of a weakened immune system. The constant stress that flows from a negative attitude also saps one's energy, focus, and motivation which ultimately lead to a state of depression, self-pity, and hopelessness.

Negative people not only harm themselves; they harm the world. Because of their low self concept they spread gloom and misery everywhere. Regrettably negative people attract other complainers. Because those who live in a world of doom and gloom alienate themselves and have no choice but to look for other negative people to associate with. They then feed off one another and get locked in a clique of losers.

Rick Nauert and John M. Grohol (2007) in their research on consumer behaviour reveal that social networks greatly influence an individual's behavior. Negative opinions cause the greatest attitude shifts, not just from good to bad, but also from bad to worse. They found that the opinions of others exert especially strong influence on individual attitudes when these opinions are negative. Furthermore, the researchers also found that those with negative opinions of the product were likely to become even more negative if asked to participate in a group discussion: When consumers expect to interact with other consumers through these forums, learning the views of these other consumers may reinforce and even polarize their opinions, making them more negative.

Co-relation between Negative Attitude and Negative emotions

Development of negative attitude towards life is more mental than physical. With negative thoughts we draw boundaries in our mind further negative life factors like a bad relationship, a history of abuse specially in early childhood, stress, frustration and poor self image can change an individual's attitude towards life which directly retards individuals overall performance. Over a period of time such tendencies become deep-rooted in mind and are nurtured by excessive negative feelings and emotions. There is a strong correlation between negative attitudes and negative emotions as both supplement and compliment each other. These negative emotions are tremendously powerful. They debilitate lives; by causing disparity in energy system, which triggers a sequence of emotional imbalance (frustration, melancholia, persistent agony, mental instability, uncontrolled anger, inferiority complex etc.), which ultimately culminates in ill health.

Negative attitude is the result of many factors. It's not an uncontrollable outcome as attitudes are subject to change. People avoid the company of those who carry around a negative attitude and seek the company of those who radiate positive attitude. No individual can expect to create a viable life space with an individual suffering from negative attitude. One must display to the world a positive attitude--even if that's not how one is feeling inside. Soon one will experience more positive things happening in one's life. Also health and surroundings will brighten up and effectiveness in life will take a quantum positive jump. Life's too short and beautiful to look at negatively and hopelessly; so make an attempt to change it, and share that ultimate happiness with others. Soon others will reach out to you.

Change of Attitude

As positive attitude synthesizes human outlook and behaviour and brings in greater harmony with the environment thus leading to greater effectiveness. It logically leads to defining the methodology of bringing about a change in individuals suffering from negative attitude syndrome, so as to make them more effective in their lives. There is a plethora of research on how to change the attitudes. It is one of the most intensely studied subjects of social psychology.

For any change to take place the individual must have the desire to change. No change can take place if the desire does not exist. In some chronic cases the resistance to change is very strong and normally the individual will adopt all defensive measures to resist change. Notwithstanding all resistance the desire to change will germinate if the mentor or a friend awakens the individual to harsh realities of his weakness. Once the individual becomes aware then his will power to change has to be put to test. Some with weak will power will require frequent reinforcements from the mentors. The individual will have to be made to demolish the boundaries drawn by him in his mind. He will have to come out of his shell and see how wonderful the world is beyond those mental blocks. Once the individual tastes this new found freedom from negativism he will start to bloom and grow.

Positive Attitude

David Baird in his e book Instant Positive Attitude writes that by adopting a positive attitude individuals begin to see the bright side of life; become optimistic and expect the best to happen, which ultimately does happen. Arun Goel while writing on the internet about the correlation between Yoga and positive attitude mentions " When we are positive, we find that our interactions with the world and ourselves become brighter, more productive and perpetuate the 'feel good' factor. This in turn makes us healthier and more peaceful." Jerry Loper (2007) advocates that human beings must develop positive attitude, positive thinking, and optimism to reap the many positive life benefits. He further goes on to explain that individuals with positive attitudes live longer, healthier and happier lives.

An unknown author mentions that there are a number of benefits that you can accrue by maintaining a positive attitude. As long as you have a good attitude, the door of success is open for you. It is beneficial to both you and others in the environment. Remez Sasson has written several articles on this subject. He writes that positive attitude helps to cope more easily with the daily affairs of life. He further elaborates that positive attitude brings in positive outlook in one's life; makes it easier to avoid worry and negative thinking. If adopted as a way of life, it generates constructive changes into one's life, and makes people happier, brighter and more successful. Positive attitude is certainly a state of mind that is well worth developing and strengthening.

Positive Thinking

Positive thinking is a mental attitude it is a mental attitude that expects good and favorable results. Positive thinking is the start point of positive attitude. It is also true that positive attitude generates positive thinking. However thought comes first; before action. The way one thinks, day in day out, affects all aspects of one's life. Thought is causal and creative, and appears in your character and life in the form of results as harmonies and antagonisms. A man thinks, and his life develops accordingly. Positive thinking admits into the mind thoughts, words and images that are conducive to growth, expansion and success while negative thinking the reverse. Based upon the stimulus a thought is generated in the mind that arouses an emotion or a feeling. This arousal could be positive or negative based on the type of thought. Positive feelings lead to attraction while negative feelings lead to repulsion. Robert A. Baron & Donn Byrne (1998). Thus it can be said that the origin of greater life space and attraction rests in positive thinking. Similar views have been expressed by Remez Sasson (2008) who writes that positive thinking leads to gaining inner peace, happiness, satisfaction, improved relationships, better health and success. He further elaborates that it also helps the daily affairs of life move more smoothly, and makes life look bright and promising. Jerry Cooper (2007) discloses that analysis of 99 Harvard graduates found a strong correlation between their positive thinking and good health later at age 40 years and above. The author further elaborates that positive attitude; positive thinking and optimism are the root cause of several good things of life.

Results of Survey

From the survey of the sampled population positive attitude is found to create up to 49.67% life space with the respondents. This is a factor that creates huge life space. It is also observed to have a positive correlation with communication and values and a negative correlation with tact charisma, personality, manipulation. Positive attitude has positive correlation with a soldier. This is followed by parents and friends in that order. With intellectual teacher and actor the correlation is positive but weak. With politician, super rich, and monarchy it is negative and in that order. It reflects that soldier, parents and friends generally display positive attitude and will thus create a healthy relationship and a larger life space in an individual's life. Communication and positive attitude too have a positive correlation implying that the two go together. A higher attitude – behaviour correlation has also been reported for persons who are highly objectively self aware. (Carver, 1975); Gibbons(1978).

A person possessing positive attitude is self aware and primarily focused on the inner self, i.e. own feelings, emotions, norms, attitudes and other internal states, whereas the attention of a person displaying negative attitude is low in self awareness and his energies are directed at other people, the personal or impersonal environment. (Hewstone, Strobe & Stephenson, 1997).

Positive Attitude and impact on Life Space Management

It is revealed through research that positive or negative thinking are contagious. People around in the environment are affected by the positive or negative vibrations that radiate from the individuals. One should develop positive attitude and radiate positive vibrations that will lead to greater harmony, peace, happiness, good health and success, and this way will cause people to like them. On the other hand people with negative attitude radiate negative aura and vibrations that create an unhealthy environment. Those who display positive attitude reflect qualities that are similar to the ones displayed by a person operating from high self concept and those who have negative attitude in life reflect low self concept. Prof SK Chakakraborty (1993) mentions that the lower self is essentially prone to pollution while the higher self is taintless. A person with positive attitude displays happiness and joy in everything. Isa Upanishad labels such behaviour as *purnata*, fullness which implies fulfillment, integrality, wholesomeness. (Swami Ranganathananda, 1993).People who operate from higher self are serene, noble , generous, fearless, humble, creative, happy and healthy, who take delight in virtues of others. People operating from lower self are selfish, jealous, destructive, irate, despondent, have great ego, fearful, mean and petty in outlook.

Those who operate from higher self create large space with others in the environment. Sound life space management brings about satisfying close relationships with friends, family or romantic partners. Establishing good relationship with others is the core of our existence as every individual wants to extend oneself to others. (Berscheid,1985, Berscheid & Peplau, 1983).Similar views have been expressed by Bram P. Buunk (1996) According to him humans find their ultimate happiness and despair in their intimate relationship. Humans compulsively seek the company of others. This attraction towards others is psychological. There are several theories that justify the principles of attraction, chief among them being the 'Reward Theory of Attraction'. (David G. Meyers, 1993). This theory is based on minimax and equity principles. Minimax principle implies that those relationships that minimize costs and give more rewards are likely to continue i.e. will minimize boredom, conflicts, expenses; maximize, self esteem, pleasure security etc. Equity principle is a sense of feeling that the outcomes people receive from a relationship are proportional to what they contribute to it. True friendship develops when concerned parties involve themselves in equitable give and take in the long term, without keeping score in the short term. David J. Schneider(1976) quotes Homans(1961), Lott & Lott (1974) and Tedeschi (1974), that positive feelings are generated towards people who reward or can reward. They further guide individuals to positively behave and respond to such people.

A very important factor that influences life space is the affective state at the time of coming in contact with others. Positive emotions generate a liking for the other person and negative emotions generate a disliking. Robert A. Baron & Donn Byrne (1998).

In Mahabharata it is said that after the great war, Lord Krishna took the Pandavas to Bheesma who lay on the bed of arrows for gaining knowledge on how to govern and rule. King Yudhistera asked Bheesma to describe the man who is dear to all and who is perfectly accomplished and endowed with all the merits. Bheesma replied that "Such a man would be learned, good and pious. His blood would not get heated by pride.

Discontent and jealousy will not be found in him. His senses will not lead him astray, and he will always have peace born of the realization of the Supreme Truth"(Kamala Subramaniam, 2004). So it emerges that a person possessing positive attitude and thoughts will be dear to all and will create a very large life space with others.

Chapter 14

Personality

Human nature is the most complex and most puzzling. Human beings not only come in various shapes and sizes but also behave very differently. To understand human nature and human being as such, a lot of research work has been carried out in various fields of life sciences, psychology, theology, philosophy, astrology, literature etc. Traditionally the definitions and beliefs about personality are myriad. Personality is derived from the Greek persona, which means mask, old Latin word persōnālitās. By the turn of the century, the new clinically inspired theories of Emil Kraeplin, Sigmund Freud, Théodule Ribot, and Pierre Janet had made personality a concept of great interest both for the psychologists and the common man. Adopted by the fraternity of psychologists in the 1920s and 1930s, the generic definition of the word personality was accepted as possession of those qualities by an individual that persist across time and contexts and that distinguish that person from all others.

The conceptual meaning of personality is multifaceted, encompassing a wide range of mental processes that influence how the person behaves across different situations. Several psychologists have defined personality differently. Carl Rogers described personality in terms of the self, an organized, permanent, subjectively perceived entity which is at the very heart of all our experiences. Gordon Allport described personality as that which an individual really is, an internal something that determines the nature of the person's interactions with the world. George Kelly regarded personality as the individuals unique way of making sense out of life experiences, while for Erik Erikson, life proceeds in terms of a series of psychological crises , with personality as a function of their outcome. (Hjelle & Ziegler,1992).

Carl Gustav Jung, (1934) described personality as "the supreme realization of the innate idiosyncrasy of a living being. It is an act of high courage flung in the face of life, the absolute affirmation of all that constitutes the individual, the most successful adaptation to the universal condition of existence coupled with the greatest possible freedom for self-determination."

Carver & Scheier (2000) define personality as a dynamic organisation, inside the person, of psychophysical systems that create a person's characteristic patterns of behaviour, thoughts, and feelings. They further suggest that the word personality conveys a sense of consistency, internal causality, and personal distinctiveness.

Theories of Personality

A lot of research work has been done on this subject; which can be classified into two streams. In one personality is viewed as a collection of distinguishable traits analysed via techniques drawn from the experimental laboratory, and in the other personality is seen as a holistic assessment of an individual's overall make-up, determined through close observation in a clinical setting. Holistic depictions of personality were investigated through the psychoanalytic depth psychology of Freud and his followers. In his psychoanalytic interpretation, Sigmund Freud (1908) asserted that the human mind could be divided into three significant components—the id, the ego, and the superego—which work together or come into conflict to shape personality.

Counter to the holistic theory has been the trait theory, which developed later during 1930s-40s, when factor analytic statistical techniques, and the development of assessment instruments such as the Minnesota Multiphasic Personality Inventory (MPPI) and the Myers-Briggs Type Indicator, allowed researchers to isolate and inter correlate particular personality variables. Studies by Raymond Cattell and Hans Eysenck have been particularly prominent in this regard. Gordon Allport delineated three kinds of traits with varying degrees of intensity: cardinal traits, central traits, and secondary traits.

Physiological or biological theories have accounted for personality primarily on the basis of physical factors, such as body type (Ernst Kretschmer, William Sheldon) or genetic make-up (Dean Hamer). Abraham Maslow and Carl Rogers supported a humanistic approach to personality, pointing out that other approaches do not factor in people's basic goodness and the motivational factors that push them toward higher levels of functioning.

Exponents of behaviourism, such as B. F. Skinner, suggest that an individual's personality is developed through external stimuli. John Carson highlights that personality thus has come to represent more external affect than internal essence. Stimulus-response or learning theories, including those of B. F. Skinner and Albert Bandura, have taken an opposite tack, explaining personality on the basis of external stimuli and the individual's responses to them. Within these theories, patterns of behaviour are believed to develop as the result of reinforcement of personal experiences or imitations of others, and differences between individuals derive from the varied sets of stimuli experienced from early childhood. This tension between the internal and the external, and between the persistent and the contextual, visible as well within psychological theory, continues to characterize notions of personality up to the present day.

Personality Development

Personality development is a lifelong phenomenon. Personality developmental concepts focus on bringing about changes in the structural and motivation of an individual's personality. Personality theories vary in the importance given to growth and changes that take place throughout life. Genetic and environmental factors must be evaluated to understand the development process. Genetic influences are transmitted from parents to the children through the mechanism of heredity. There is ample evidence based on study of twins that emotional stability, extraversion altruism and shyness are strongly heritable. Also parents serve as role models and children adopt several styles of behaviour from them, which they continue to emulate for rest of their lives. Hjelle & Ziegler (1992). Man is as much a biological as well a social organism. The role of genetic and maturation process starts from the embryonic stage and continues for the rest of life. Presently lesser attention is paid to biological and genetic aspects of personality development as compared to psychological aspects. Stage theories focus on the impact of critical or central happenings at different times in life on personality and cognitive development. Kohlberg (1969) is of the opinion that cognitive structures serve to change stimulus inputs and that in turn changes the cognitive structures. Stage theories suggest that there are distinct qualitative differences in personality at different ages (Walter Mischel, 1971).

Every Individual aspires to cultivate and acquire a personality that will be attractive and thus improve individual's acceptance in his desired environment. No one appreciates a negative or unattractive personality. Every individual must therefore attempt to make one's personality as pleasing and attractive as possible. Aim should be to develop a healthy and positive personality. People with healthy personality are those who have inner harmony, and are at peace with themselves and with others. They have the capability to realistically carry out appraisal of the self, and of the situation. They are goal oriented and have greater social acceptance. They operate from their higher self, are well adjusted and are productive part of the society. (Hurlock, 1976). Self actualized people have been rated as healthy and spiritually inclined personalities by Maslov also.

Roger Highfield (2007),a science editor, in his article "Personality more attractive than looks," mentions that the psychologists who conducted the research work on the subject, had come to the conclusion that how a partner acts and not looks, is more important to both men and women who want to settle down. He further elaborates that this pattern may be indicative of the greater importance of a positive personality for a long-term relationship for both sexes. While the world consists of mere mortals who exist at the physical plane of existence. In this plane a great amount of importance is given by the individuals to physical aspects of personality development. The whole world of film and fashion industry thrives on this singular element of personality presentation. All actors and models invest their time and money to keep themsrlves physically fit and attractive. Some tips that can add value to physical dimension of personality are by facing the world firmly and squarely. This should be done by holding up the head and keeping the eyes well to the front. A study of men discloses the fact that the strong men never tilt the head. Their heads sit perfectly straight on strong necks. Another important part of personality is carriage or physical bearing of the person. A person must be physically neat and clean. No one likes the presence and company of dirty people. Voice too plays a major role in presentation of a personality. A man having a well controlled, even, pleasant voice has an advantage over others having equal abilities in other aspects of personality, but lacking that one quality. The value of a vibrant, resonant, soft and flexible voice is great asset. Obese persons are not considered attractive. There are grooming classes held to improve dressing sense and conduct of individuals. Proper dressing sense adds value to physical attractiveness. An ill fitting or shabby or dirty dress is not appreciated. It negatively influences the personality of a person.

Another aspect of development of physical attractiveness is based on physical grooming. Several studies have shown that regular exercise over a period of several years can change personality by increasing vitality; improving patience and humour, and by making a person better tempered and more easy-going. They also show that high levels of fitness are often associated with high levels of self-assurance, self-confidence, and emotional stability. These studies refer to ordinary people. Film actors and sportsperson, whose bread and butter are dependent on their physical charm and strength; spend valuable time, money and energy in gymnasiums.

A valuable aspect of personality is that of self respect. If you have real self respect it will manifest itself in your outward demeanor and appearance. One must endeavour to develop self respect and must not demean oneself for that will lead to strengthening of the lower self. Similar views are aired in Bhagwad Gita. Sloka 5 of Chapter 6, that states that "One should lift oneself by one's own efforts and should not degrade oneself; for one's own self is ones friend and one's own self is ones enemy." Also self-control particularly in the matter of keeping anger under check is an important dimension of personality development. Anger is a mark of weakness, not of strength. The man who loses his temper immediately places himself at a disadvantage. Individuals must cultivate a quiet and serene disposition towards the world. Another dimension of personality worth cultivating is the art of taking interest in others. Others are drawn towards those who show genuine interest in them. Vast majority of the people in this world are so engrossed in their own affairs that they convey the impression of being "apart" and aloof from others with whom they come in contact. This mental state manifests in a most unpleasant and negative form of personality. This taking interest in others manifests itself in many ways; one of the chief means is by being a good listener. A human being wants to be heard. Half the world problems are resolved when an individual has a positive listener in attendance. Therefore listen with genuine interest. Be careful not to bore people with your own personal experiences.

Individuals can change their personality by sheer will. Before ignition of the change a desire for change must germinate. Change gets facilitated when the individual desires the change. After accepting the necessity for change an individual must carry out SWOT (Strength, weakness, opportunity and threats) analysis of one's own personality. This analysis will reveal the type of personality individual should have. Individual should then make a good mental pattern or mould of the desired personality to be developed; and in that mould pour in the desired mental material steadily. From the mould will then come forth the character and personality that individual desires. Thereafter it only needs to be polished and presented.

A well balanced personality is chracterised by proper insight and understanding of the real self through proper self knowledge and evaluation. Also a well adjusted personality is self actualized and finds joy and happiness in his work. To achieve such a positive healthy personality which is balanced and wholesome, all aspects of the psychophysical organism, physical, psychical, social or super individualistic must be coordinated into a balanced and harmonious whole in relationship with the environment. For attainment of such a balanced personality individual efforts are a must. Normally there is evidence of inertia and maintenance of status quo. (Uday Shankar , 1980).

Relevance to Life Space management

Survey results reveal that a good personality can create up to 41.7% life space with them. A good healthy charismatic personality acts like a magnet and creates a large life space for itself with others. Charismatic personalities are of two types; those who radiate positive charisma and those who display negative charisma. Negative charismatic personalities create transitory life space which is short lived, while positive healthy personality creates a long term life space. While analyzing various celebrity personalities how well they create life space with Indian population; it emerges that Swami Vivekananda creates the largest life space followed by Dr Homi Bhaba, Smt Indira Gandhi, Sai Baba, Azmi Premji, Sachin Tendulkar, Dhyan Chand, Aishwarya Rai Madhubala and Lalu Prasad Yadav in that order. The quantum of relative space created by the celebrities as revealed from survey in percentage is as tabulated below:-

CELEBRITIES	COMBINED	RANKING
Swami Vivekanand	46.30%	1
Dr Homi bhaba	37.40%	2
Indira Gandhi	35.95%	3
Sachin Tendulkar	34.40%	4
Sai Baba Puthaparti	33.94%	5
Azmi Premji	31.95%	6
Dhyan Chand	31.23%	7
Aishwarya Rai	27.29%	8
Madhubala	23.55%	9
Lalu Prasad Yadav	16.80%	10

Table 2 Life space created by various celebrities

From the above it is evident that in Indian context personality that radiates spirituality, character, love, intelligence/ wisdom, is friendly and caring creates a larger and lasting life space. It is the internal strengths and not the external physical beauty, wealth and other parameters that create lasting life space. Culturally Indian citizen shows greater reverence to spiritually inclined people. As per Indian culture spiritual guru and parents are revered most. In fact Kabir highlights the relevance of Guru in his famous saakhi. " *Guru Govind Dou Khare, Kaake Laagoon Paanye. Balihari Guru Aapne, Govind Diyo Bataaye.*" Guru and Govind both stand before me, whose feet should I touch first? Blessed be Guru mine, who caused with God my tryst. (Jigyasu, 2005). Any person who is endowed with such spiritual traits is most sought after by the world.

Chapter 15

Tact

So many times in our lives we are thrown into situations that need to be handled with care otherwise the situation may lead to embarrassment and unproductive outcome. Tact is a good tool to deal with such situations. Regrettably everyone does not possess this trait, which is so essential for enhancing individual and organizational effectiveness. Tact is derived from old French, sense of touch, from Latin *tactus*, from *tangere* to touch. Tact implies delicate and considerate perception of what is appropriate. Some of the synonyms of tact are address, poise, diplomacy, savoir-faire. All these words reflect the ability to deal with others with skill, sensitivity, and finesse. The word address reflects communication skill and grace in dealing with new and trying social situations and may imply success in attaining one's ends Poise implies both tact and address but stresses self-possession and ease in meeting difficult situations. Diplomacy represents skillful management of difficult or embarrassing situations. Savoir-faire denotes having worldly experience and a sure awareness of knowing and speaking the right or graceful things.

Tact has been described as acute sensitivity to what is proper and appropriate in dealing with others, including the ability to speak or act without offending them. Basically it implies propriety and the ability to speak or act inoffensively. The pocket Oxford dictionary describes tact as 'Delicate perception of the right thing to do or say, adroitness in dealing with others or with difficulties due to personal feeling.' (Fowler & Fowler, 1961). While The American Heritage Dictionary (2003) of the English Language describes tact as 'a sense of the best and most considerate way to deal with people so as not to upset them and the skill in handling difficult situations·

Developing Tact

From the various definitions given above it clearly emerges that tact is a transaction of good sense in our communication and behaviour to maintain good healthy relations. Tact is also an aspect of communication by both verbal or nonverbal means. Like all communication skills tact too can be learnt and developed. Certain aspects that need attention while developing tact are enumerated below:-

a. **Develop communication Skills:** Analyse the misunderstandings and miscommunications that have crippled the relationships. Change methods of communicating that create such misunderstandings. Learn and master diplomacy. Learn and use the right words. Avoid words and phrases that rob the message of its credibility. Identify and know exactly what to say and when. Never use and say wrong words. Convey the exact message.

b. **Be calm:** Learn to control emotions and anger. Words and actions spoken or done in anger are generally irrational, abusive and damaging. Cool down heated verbal exchanges before situations get out of control. In an argument he wins who maintains his calm. Remember an old maxim "One silence can kill a hundred arguments". Thus one can deal more effectively with those who challenge authority or simply irritate one if one maintains his calm. Smooth over hard feelings and prevent grudges from being formed with damage control tactics

c. **Be a good listener:** Only he who is a good listener is also a good communicator. Everyone wants to be heard and listened to. No one likes interference while they speak. It is in fact bad manners and form to interfere and stop others while they are talking. Listen and communicate with empathy. The other person will be sold out on you. The more other person talks the more he reveals his true nature.

d. **Learn to deliver bad news:** There will be occasions in one's life when bad news has to be communicated to others. The problem becomes more acute and complex when they are near and dear ones. Also learn to say no, without hurting the feelings of others.

e. **Be positive:** A positive person creates the right ambience for good relationships. A positive person easily develops consensus, and easily gets things done with tact and finesse.

f. **Empathy:** Empathy is the basis for tact, says Cheryl Park, coordinator of early childhood education for Cambrian College in Sudbury, Ontario. A tactful person is able to understand how other people might feel, by placing himself in their shoes and with that understanding he avoids hurting their feelings. (Holly Bennet, May 2008). On the other hand convey something of immediate or long range benefit to, or value to the other person. (Leyton, 1970).

Relevance to the Study

From survey it emerges that tact can create up to 30.96% life space with people. Tactful people are successful in creating the right environment for future relationships. Diplomacy an aspect of tact is used internationally to smoothen out conflicts and enhance good relations with other countries. Even in business tactful negotiators are employed to clinch business deals. Correlation of tact with other parameters of life space and other people is given in the various tables as shown below:-

PARAM-ETERS	Tact	Commu-nication	Manipu-lation	Charac-ter	Positive attitude	Values
Pearson Cor-relation	1	0.182483	0.154517	-0.11803	-0.13127	-0.2297
Sig. (2-tailed)	_	0.001251	0.006412	0.037795	0.020989	4.45E-05
Sum of Squares and Cross-prod-ucts	1200.4	254.2	249.4	-144.2	-150.359	-338.2
Covariance	3.88479	0.822654	0.80712	-0.46667	-0.48818	-1.0945
N	310	310	310	310	309	310

Table 3 Relevant correlation of tact with other parameters of life space

Non parametric spearmans correlation with other people is as shown below:-

	Tact	Politician	SuperRich	King / queen	Parents
Correlation Coefficient	1	0.233522757	0.245697798	0.177494	-0.13584
Sig. (2-tailed)	.	3.28808E-05	1.21022E-05	0.001704	0.016705
N	310	310	310	310	310

Table 4 Correlation of tact with other people and celebrities

From the correlation details of the survey it emerges that tact has a positive correlation with communication and manipulation and a negative correlation with values, positive attitude, and character in that order. It only justifies that tact is an aspect of communication and manipulation. When tact is employed to manipulate it is viewed negatively and hence it has negative correlation with values, positive attitude and character. Tact when used positively creates reasonable amount of lasting life space. With other people it is found to have positive correlation with super rich, politician and king/queen in that order and a negative correlation with parents. Super rich, politicians and king and queen seem to be more adept at being tactful while parents are by and large very forthright in dealing with their children. As tact is generally viewed negatively it does not create as much space as the other factors create at individual level. It is recommended that it should be viewed as an aspect of communication.

Chapter 16

Respect

Every human being aspires to be respected. There is a popular saying that respect has to be earned; which implies that one has to work towards attaining respect. Respectfulness is essential for creating a harmonious relationship with family, friends and all other people in society. Respect is a natural response of civility which as mentioned earlier cannot be demanded. Respect shows consideration for another, implying that others' thoughts and desires are factored into our planning and decision making while dealing with the other person.

The word respect is derived from Middle English, regard, from Latin respectus, from past participle of respicere, to look back at, regard. The meaning of respect has been interpreted by the American Heritage Dictionary(2003) as, to feel or show deferential regard for; esteem. A feeling of; appreciative, often deferential regard; and esteem. The state of being regarded with honour or esteem. Willingness to show consideration or appreciation. Polite expressions of consideration or deference: pay one's respects.

Wikipedia, the free encyclopedia has covered the subject of respect in greater detail. It highlights that by showing respect to others it adds general reliability to social relations; and it helps people to get along with each other in society. Each society and culture has its own norms of showing respect to others. In many European cultures, people shake hands. In others, such as in Japan people bow at the waist when meeting. In India they join hands and with folded hands show respect to the others. Also they touch the feet of elders as a mark of respect and the elders bless them as a mark of their love and affection for the young. World over sign of respect in almost any form of the military is a salute. A salute is used by a subordinate to show respect to his superior officers who in turn reciprocates with a salute.

How to Gain Respect

Not all people are respected, though everyone desires the same. While analyzing the difference between those who are admired and respected and those who are not it emerges the difference is in certain qualities of personality which can be developed. At work place or at home or in any given environment it is vital to earn the respect of the people you are interacting with. If you have their respect, they will work harder and longer to help you reach your aims and objectives. Some of the qualities and steps that can enhance an individual's respect amongst others are listed below:-

a. **Serve the People:** Serve others from the core of your heart, by making sure you are doing everything you can to address their concerns and improve their welfare. Good deeds will be rewarded; there is no need to force the issue. Respect often comes to those who don't chase after it.

b. **Have confidence in your Abilities:** People respect those who know their job, as well as the jobs of the people they lead, thoroughly and with confidence. To gain the respect of others, it is important to have faith in yourself. This is not an egotistical pride, but modest self respect and faith in your inner capacities.

c. **Respect Others:** Respect begets respect. We must learn to accept people as they are and respect them for what they are. Then people will respect us. We must learn to respect people who are elder to us and more experienced. Every family, society, organization and culture has its own norms of displaying respect and we must follow those norms to convey our respects.

d. **Listen More Talk Less:** Everyone likes to listen to their own voice. Therefore patiently listen to others they will appreciate your concern and attention. By listening you can find out what their wants, needs, skills, aspirations and frustrations are. We do not command respect by excessively talking. The oft repeated saying 'actions speak louder than words' is very applicable here. If we are judicious in speaking people will give more importance to our words.

e. **Honesty:** Be cent percent honest in life for there is no partial honesty. An individual is either honest or dishonest. There are no shades of grey in this value. The importance of honesty cannot be underestimated. A liar will never be able to gain respect anywhere. When things go wrong there is a temptation to look for someone or something to blame. It takes a certain amount of courage to just be honest and accept things that didn't work out as planned; in the long run, this honesty will be appreciated. Honesty will earn the trust of the people you are leading.

f. Equanimity: Vedanta preaches equanimity. To gain the genuine respect of others it is important to be detached from dualities of life like praise and criticism. Praise can easily go to our head and bloat our ego and pride; this diminishes all the good work we have done before. On the opposite side, we should not get flustered by criticism. There is a great dignity in being able to be composed and not to be moved by both praise and criticism. If we can maintain this highest principle despite all provocations, people will come to appreciate and respect us. (Tejvan Pettinger, Feb 2008).

g. Honour and Dignity: These are the fall outs of respect. Soldiers will lay down their life for Honour. Heroes the world over strive for honour and dignity. We must respect such heroes and emulate them in all our actions.

h. Humility: Humility earns respect. Humility emerges from a pure heart that has no ego. Such a person is revered the world over.

Relevance to the Study

Respect is considered as a synonym for politeness or manners. Respect is basically an attitude that is shown towards any individuals' feelings or interest. It is acknowledging another's feelings in any kind of relationship. It may not necessarily be feelings shared between individuals but could also be referred to animals, groups or between countries. It implies to the phrase 'treat others the way you want to be treated.' By being courteous and respectful we create reasonable space with others. From the study of the responses of the respondents it is evident that respect plays a great role in creating life space especially with our parents, elders and spouse. With our parents and elders it emerges that respect is number Uno life space creator. The top ten creators of life space at domestic environment are as shown in the table given below. Respect has been shown highlighted in box.

Spouse		Children		Parents		Friends		Total	
Item	score	Item	score	Item	score	Item	score	Item	score
Commu-nication	127	love/affection	138	Respect	119	Com-munica-tion	131	Com-munica-tion	462
Love	89	values	105	Commu-nication	105	charac-ter	57	love/affection	301
Faith	48	Commu-ication	99	caring	105	help	55	values	255
Under-standing	47	care	81	values	80	attitude	50	care	230
Respect	43	advce/guide	47	love/affection	58	values	36	Respect	195
Positive attitude	35	character	41	self cont/mgt	48	person-ality	35	charac-ter	179
Values	34	under-standing	26	character	48	Respect	27	attitude	126
character	33	Self Man-agement	24	Under-standing	23	Under-standing	26	Under-standing	122
Care	30	friend	24	help	23	tact	26	self cont/mgt	110
Sharing	29	tact	23	Positive attitude	21	sharing	21	help	96

Table 5 Respect as it emerges in the surveyed data

From the details obtained from the survey respect ranks as number five in creating life space. It is sufficient to deduce that respect is one of the major factors that create life space with an individual. Individuals must respect others for what they are and they will be able to create sizeable life space with others in the environment.

Chapter 17

Self Management

Success comes to those who have self control and are able to manage the self. While self control is understood as the control of gratification of senses, self management means different things in different fields. In our study self management implies application of methods, skills, and strategies by which individuals can effectively direct their own activities toward the achievement of individual objectives. This is achieved by goal setting, planning, and scheduling for self-intervention and self development. Self control and self management go hand in hand. If there is no self control then there can be no self management and vice versa. Self control is the start point of self management. People demonstrate great differences in the level of self-control and self management. Self control can be affected due to physical ailment or past experiences and weak or strong will power. Self control can be improved throughout the course of life. Some developmental psychologists argue that this is normal, as people age from infant to adulthood .Though this may sound normal quite a few do not learn self control throughout their lives. Self control must be learnt from childhood and this must become a matter of habit.

Self Control

In layman's language self control is the ability to control oneself. Self-control is the ability to constrain what one does so that the individual might accomplish some higher goal. Self control is the ability to delay immediate gratification by self imposed will power. (Walter Mischel, 1971). Immediate gratification is felt through impulses. Freud called it id. Self control is also the control of impulses; which is the central task of psychological system we call personality. Freud conceived of impulse control as a function of the ego. (Caprara & Cervone, 2000).

Thesaurus defines self control as keeping of one's thoughts and emotions to oneself as also willpower over one's actions. In philosophy dictionary it is defined as the quality of mind with which we resist temptations and do not succumb to them. In Sports Science and Medicine it is described as the ability to exercise control over one's own feelings and behaviour. A more appropriate definition is given by Wikipedia dictionary which defines it as control of one's emotions, desires, or actions by one's own will.

Self-control accepts that others are more important than self. They learn how to put off fulfilling their own interests so that they can serve others. A free and orderly society can only be built with this quality. Without it, man is unable to follow his conscience or the rules of a society. There is no freedom without self-control for uncontrolled man is convinced his desires are more important than the needs of others and will oppress others to fulfill those desires. Several behavioural scientists have researched on the subject of self control, the most prominent amongst them being Walter Mischel.

Around 1970, psychologist Walter Mischel   carried out the famous "Marshmallow", experiment with four year old children. He left these kids in a room with a bell and marshmallows. If they rang the bell, he would come back and they could eat the marshmallow. If, however, they didn't ring the bell and waited for him to come back on his own, they could then have two marshmallows. In videos of the experiment, the children were observed squirming, kicking, hiding their eyes -- desperately trying to exercise self-control so that they could wait and get two marshmallows. Their performance varied widely. Some broke down and rang the bell within a minute. Others lasted 15 minutes. These children were thereafter tracked by Walter Mischel. It was observed by him that those children, who waited longer, went on to get higher SAT scores. They got into better colleges and had, on average, better adult outcomes. The children who rang the bell quickest went on to become bullies. They received worse teacher and parental evaluations. Some of them had drug problems by the time they were 32 years old. Since self control emerged as delay of gratification Mischel carried out several other experiments on effects of delay on gratification. He used live adult models to display gratification which was contrary to what the children had displayed. Thereafter the models also made explanatory statements about their choices. The children were influenced by the live adult models and changed their gratification accordingly (Mischel, 1971).

From the Mischel's experiment it emerges that self control must be taught from childhood. It is the responsibility of parents to teach their children self control. Parents and elders can influence the self control mechanism for delay of gratification in children. In modern times we helplessly watch parents weaken the self control mechanism by giving to their children more than what is required by the child. If the child asks for a mobile phone the parents will give the latest and most expensive i-phone. If the child asks for a laptop the parents will give the latest i-pad. Some parents feel that this is a good way to display their love for the child. What they do not understand is that by going overboard they are reducing the child's self control mechanism which in the long run will harm the child. Self-control is an essential building block to the creation of great men and women. It is most frustrating when parents discover that their child's behaviour is out of control, and they do not know what to do about it. Some people view this form of child behavioural aberration as an expression of independence Vast majority of parents reconcile and put up with their out-of-control child, perhaps thinking nothing much can be done. The fact is self-control plays an important part in all of our lives. We can't live without it. Self-control is easily developed when the child is small, but as adults we know things are much harder to change.

Parents must understand that development of child is their basic responsibility. The earlier they start training their children, the better it will be for all concerned Developing self-control in children is an essential part of caring. Self-control is learned quickly when parents consistently combine positive encouragement with chastisement.

Developing Self Control

Self-control can be developed by enhancing both cognitive and behavioral skills to maintain self-motivation and achieve personal goals. F. Skinner in 'Science and Human Behaviour' prescribes nine methods of developing self control. These are as given below:-

a. **Physical Restraint and physical aid:** The basic principle is to manipulate the physical environment to make some response easier to physically execute and others physically more difficult; to affect and impinge on behavioural outcome.

b. **Changing the stimulus:** This involves manipulating the stimulus by removing distractions, or hiding temptations or just the occasion to change the behaviour.

c. **Depriving and satiating:** This involves manipulating one's behaviour by delaying or depriving one's gratification.

d. **Manipulating emotional conditions:** This involves removing the emotional stimuli by change of scene.

e. **Using aversive stimulation:** This implies that an individual uses aversive control by doing certain things the individual becomes more aware of the happening.

f. **Drugs:** Prescribed or self administered drugs may be used to simulate changes in ones conditioning history. (This should be used as a last resort.)

g. **Operant conditioning:** Methods or techniques that are unique to operant conditioning may be used as a special form of self-control.

h. **Punishment:** Self-punishment is imposed to reduce the probability of future behaviour.

i. **Doing something else:** Skinner mentions that by 'doing something else' or more specifically something that is incompatible with our response we bring about a behavioural change by which our responses are more in our control. He further elaborates it by highlighting that Jesus exemplified this principle by loving his enemies.

Some other methods of developing self control are as given below:-

a. **Antardrishti:** It is the ability to look within. Everyone should spend some time on the self and identify own strengths and weaknesses. Ideally carry out SWOT analysis and find out ways to improve the self.

b. **Antarmukhita:** This is the ability to talk to the self. Through a self dialogue one should do atma vishleshan or analysis of the area in which one is lacking control and then build upon it. Remember in terms of gaining self control, knowledge really is power.

   c.   **Antarshuddhi:** It is the abilty to cleanse oneself of one's weaknesses. After analysis of your weaknesses you must practice self-denial. Challenge yourself to break your old destructive habits as also ask others to challenge you to break your habits. Stay accountable to someone. This feedback mechanism reinforces self control habits.

Basically development of self control is dependent on three factors, i.e. environmental, behavioural and cognitive. Environmental factors will involve changing or avoiding the group, time, events places, or situations which lead to problematic behaviour. Behavioural strategies involve changing the antecedents or consequences of a behaviour. Cognitive factors focus on changing one's beliefs by using self-instructions, using NLP techniques, by positive reinforcements etc.

The goal of self-control is to reduce behavioural excesses or deficiencies. Behavioral deficiencies occur when an individual does not engage in a positive, desirable behaviour frequently enough. Behavioural excesses on the other hand occur when an individual engages in negative, undesirable behaviour too often. Both behavioural deficiencies and excesses reflect negativity in the personality and are destructive and harmful in the long run. Albert Bandura has covered this subject of relevance of self control in social cognitive theory. According to him one's behavior is influenced by several factors, including one's own thoughts and beliefs, and the environment. In determining which behaviours an individual will attempt to change, Bandura mentions this will depend on the individual's beliefs, outcome expectancies, and self control at the given time·

Ideally self control is developed by self denial. One must have lesser attachments and must learn to give away things. Self control should be a lifelong obsession. Therefore make self-denial a habit and not just a trend. No long term change can come about without the will to change. Therefore one must possess a strong will power. Without a strong will power an individual from time to time will keep on punishing oneself for the lack of control. This will be damaging as it will only feed the power of one's lack of self control.

Every religion too emphasises on self control. . In the Bible, Paul the Apostle describes self control as one of the fruits of the Holy Spirit. He further instructs the younger men to be self controlled. Peter too emphasises on self control and describes it as the basic requirement for the salvation of a Christian (2 Peter 1:5-8). According to Buddhist philosophy,

Dhammapada 80 and 145 highlight that the virtuous control themselves. In Chandogya Upanishad the teacher tells the disciple 'Tat Tvam Asi'; That Thou Art, the whole universe is centered in the Self. The Upanishads tell man that he is not finite, That he is not limited because he views himself through the limitations of the body and senses. Further in Isa Upanishad it is mentioned that grief comes to those who identify themselves with the limitations of the body and mind.(Swami Ranganathananda, 1993). Sri Aurobindo (1998) mentions that human feelings and their actions are controlled by their *prakriti* mostly by their vital and physical nature. While man who is endowed with a mind tries to control his vital and physical nature the control is partial as man is deluded by vital and physical desires. He further elaborates that self control can be developed through increased will power and sadhana. It is through sadhana that the higher nature of man works within the psychic and spiritual being. Guru Nanak Dev also echoes similar sentiments when he says that victory over the self is victory over the world. (Jap, 6). He further preaches that one should set one's affairs straight by one's own hands. (Asa, 474). (Harnam Singh Shan,2002).

Most of the research in the field of self control reflects that self control is also influenced by culture. Cultures across the globe vary in terms of the experiences they provided to the people who are a part of these cultures. Logue mentions that it is possible, therefore, that during development, people in different cultures acquire different styles and techniques of self-control. Louge further states that, self-control and resistance to temptation has long been part of Americans' Judeo-Christian heritage. Whereas in oriental cultures, self-control is viewed as being achieved by yielding, letting go, acceptance, and non-attachment. This difference between the Western society and Eastern society is not due to descriptions of self-control but rather due to the differences in what is considered a large outcome worth exhibiting self-control for. However with growing technology and globalization, differences between the two cultures is narrowing down·

Self Management

In recent years, the term "self-management" has replaced "self-control," because self-control implies changing behaviour through sheer willpower. Self-management, on the other hand, involves becoming aware of the natural processes that affect a particular behaviour and consciously altering those processes, resulting in the desired behavioural change.

Self-management means different things in different fields: In organisations, self management means that members within the group manage their own affairs. There is no dedicated authority to give orders and take care of others. The employees or workers themselves manage issues like customer care, general production methods, scheduling, division of labor etc; instead of the traditional authoritative supervisor telling workers what, where and how to do. In business, education and psychology, self-management refers to methods, skills, and strategies that individuals employ to carry out self analysis / evaluation, and set their goals and objectives in life. It also includes planning and execution of the strategies for self development. In the field of computer science, it refers to the process by which computer systems will manage their own operation without human intervention. Self-Management technologies will soon pervade the next generation of network management systems. In the medical field due to paucity of medical staff at all places self-management assumes great importance. It means the interventions, training, and skills by which patients with a chronic condition, disability, or disease can effectively take care of themselves. In Housing colonies or societies, it refers to management of the colony or housing society either through an elected committee structure, or through a Board of Directors that has management as well as executive functions.

Self Management Strategies

For creating self management environment the following strategies are recommended:-

a. **Plan:** This is the basic principle of management. By planning there is objectivity and predictability otherwise you are neither here nor there. There is therefore a need for an individual to organize the environment and plan for the day, week, month, year and entire life activities.

b. **Management of Time:** This is one asset on which no one has control. This asset should be managed otherwise will be wasted out. In our life everything has a relevance related to time. If actions are not taken in time their relevance and importance is lost out. Based on our plan objectives of life can be accomplished if they are prioritized and taken seriously enough to get them done in a timely manner. Time management skills boil down to awareness, organization and commitment. Awareness part of time management corresponds to self- management and monitoring methods of our efforts on habit change.

c. **Questioning & Feedback:** Feedback and questioning are the basic tenant of gaining knowledge about what needs to be improved and how.   Make it a habit to seek feedback and question why an act ought to be done.

d. **Listening:** Proper feedback comes by listening. Listen to the sane advice of others as also one's inner voice.

e. **Focus:** Concentrate on your aim and objectives of self improvement and management for success comes to those who are focused.

f. **Faith in Self:** Throughout the history of mankind faith in self has been the most potent motive in lives of all great people of the world. As per Swami Vivekananda all the differences between man and man is owing to the existence or non existence of faith in self. Learn never to say NO or I CANNOT; for you are infinite. (Myren & Madison, 2001).

g. **Perseverance:** Change in mannerism and habits can take place if the desire to change is constantly practiced. Lack of will in execution shall limit the growth of man. One has to be focused and persevere to achieve the desired change. From time to time one must put the will power to test.

Edward J. O'Keefe & Donna S. Berger, in an article in internet advice the students' to improve their self management techniques by managing their ABCs i.e. Affect, Behaviour and Cognition by focusing on the following:-

a. Increase motivation

b. End procrastination and save time.

c. Improve performance in class by obtaining better grades.

d. Improve interpersonal relationship.

e. Improve communication skills.

f. Improve self confidence.

g. Develop positive thoughts, feelings, attitude and behaviour.

Results of Study

From the surveyed data it is revealed that self management has a very weak and negligible correlation with other factors of life space. Similarly it has a very weak and negligible correlation with various types of people one interacts in the environment. From the survey it is evident that while self control only affects the individual it does not affect other people and hence there is a weak correlation with others. Any individual who lacks self control or is not able to manage own affairs is unlikely to create any viable life space with others. Self management or self control on its own may not generate life space, but self control/ management is instrumental in developing a personality with values, character and positive attitude. Therefore indirectly it is an essential ingredient for creating life space. From the survey it emerges that the quantum of life space in percentage that self control / management can create as an independent parameter is substantial 40 .69 %. Comparative details are as given below:-

Parameters	Percentage
Positive attitude	49.67
Communication	46.44
Character	45.06
Personality	41.7
Values	41.6
Self Management	**40.69**
Tact	30.96
Charisma	25.14
Manipulation	21.83

Table 6 At Individual level quantum of life space created in percentage

Chapter 18

Manipulation

The word manipulation or manipulator generates negative thoughts and feelings. Nobody wants to be manipulated. It is noted that managers, as do other people, manipulate their subordinates or colleagues by exploiting their psychological needs. There are benefits if it leads to enhanced performance; and potential hazards when people are manipulated to do wrong things. The danger thus with manipulation is that people can be lead to do immoral acts. History is full of examples where people were manipulated to do wrong things. The greatest example in modern history is Hitler's manipulation of the German people. Later, many people regretted doing this. Psychological manipulation is a very powerful tool, which can be used both for productive and destructive reasons. There seems to be some similarity between management and manipulation, as management according to some wise people is nothing but pure manipulation of human and other resources. The pocket Oxford Dictionary of current English defines the word manage as 'Conduct the working of , have effective control of, bend to one's will, cajole, find a way, contrive, bring about, secure.' It further defines management as skillful handling, cajolery. Cajolery is described as persuade or soothe by flattery or deceit. Manipulation is described as 'handle (instrument & c), deal skillfully with, arrange dexterously, and manage tactfully or craftily, (facts, subject, statistics, person or his emotions. (Fowler & Fowler,1961).From the meanings described of these words the negativity emerges in all three words and hence the similarity.

Manipulation is derived from the French word manipule, (meaning handful, as of grain), and from Latin word manipulus,(sheaf, handful). Manipulation has been described differently in different fields. Normal dictionary defines it as 'The act or practice of manipulating, the state of being manipulated. Shrewd or devious management, especially to one's own advantage. The other definitions are as shown in succeeding paragraphs:-.

Investment Dictionary: It describes manipulation as the act of artificially inflating or deflating the price of a security. This is also known as "price manipulation". In most economies world over manipulation is illegal and have thus instituted several protection mechanism specially post Enron Securities scam in USA. Similar views are given in Financial; & Investment Dictionary where manipulation is described as being carried out by buying or selling shares to create a false impression of active trading and thus influence other investors to buy or sell shares. Those found guilty of manipulation are subject to criminal and civil penalties.

Political Dictionary: Manipulation implies turning of a situation to advantage like it is amply witnessed in India whenever there is a hung parliament. This may be by use of procedural devices such as changing the order of the agenda or the voting rules, or introducing new proposals not for their merits but to cause split in rival camp.

Collaborative International Dictionary of English: Manipulation is the act or process of manipulating, or the state of being manipulated; the act of handling work by hand; use of the hands in an artistic or skillful manner, in science or art.

Webster: The use of the hands in mesmeric operations. Artful management; as the manipulation of political bodies; sometimes, a management or treatment for purposes of deception or fraud.

WordNet (2005): Manipulation is exerting shrewd or devious influence especially for one's own advantage; the action of touching with the hands (or the skillful use of the hands) or by the use of mechanical means.

Manipulation Techniques:

It is said that all great people have been great manipulators too. They could manipulate the changes in human outlook and behaviour and make people more productive part of the society or organisation. Manipulation like any skill can be acquired. Also skills and techniques to guard against negative manipulation can be acquired and learnt. According to behavioral psychologist Abraham Maslow, you can influence people to do what you want them to do by appealing to their core needs and motivations. Tricking people into doing what you want them to do is much simpler than it may seem- all it takes is a general understanding of the needs of people, how they make their decisions and act or behave to fulfill those needs. The trick is to offer a hungry man a loaf of bread and he will do what you want him to do. Politicians, the world over use this stratagem to remain in power. Salesmen too use this tool very effectively.

George K. Simon, Jr., in his book "In Sheeps Clothing: Understanding and Dealing with Manipulative People", has identified five traits that a manipulator will exploit. The first is naiveté. Manipulator identifies a naiveté person and takes advantage of him by lying about his own intentions and behaviour by presenting himself as a person of character that can be trusted. Having won the trust he will manipulate the other person to accept the rationalizations and lies that he presents than to believe the contrary evidence. The second and third traits Simon mentions are over-conscientiousness and low self-confidence. Basically it implies that certain people take things to heart easily and come down harder on themselves. They will always give others the benefit of the doubt, especially when the manipulator accuses them of having been at fault or having bad intentions. This lack of self confidence in own judgments prevents one from acting or speaking up. This weakness is exploited by the manipulator. The fourth trait Simon mentions is over-intellectualization. In this case the victim of manipulation instead of averting the situation tries to focus his or her attention on understanding the roots of the troublesome behaviour of the manipulator and how he might be able to help change such behaviours. The fifth trait is emotional dependency. Here Simon refers to a personality that tends to be submissive and overly-compliant. A manipulator uses threats of abandonment or withdrawal of love as a weapon against this kind of personality. Some other techniques that a manipulator may use are listed below:-

a.   **Flattery:** The greatest known weakness of a person is to hear own praise. Flattery therefore becomes a powerful tool in hands of a manipulator. The flatterer will pay extra attention and make the victim feel special and a part of the 'inner circle'. Having won the trust of the victim manipulator will then exploit the weaknesses and needs of the victim to his own advantage.

b.   **Gossip:** Gossip is a major covert tool in the hands of a manipulator. A lot of half truths can be transmitted through this medium. Women, in particular, are targeted with gossip, knowing that men will sometimes hear and believe things from their wives or paramours that they would find inappropriate to hear from others.

c. **Isolation:** Manipulators isolate their victims to limit all contrary influences. They will attempt to create an inclusive group and propagate to mistrust others who are not part of the group. This group is projected as the elite group of which the victim is privileged to be included as a member. This elitism is used to control dissent and thus manipulation becomes easier.

d. **Confusion and Group Think:** Manipulators often create a group lingo, or special vocabulary that sounds foreign to outsiders. These words could be crazy sounding and are often not well-defined, but no one is willing to admit that they do not understand the meaning of these words. The result is a quiet confusion. It also creates a group think mentality where everyone feels he is the true follower and not its leader.

e. **Pity:** This is a very effective tool in manipulating people with normal capacities for caring and compassion. Manipulators present a moving, miserable   and tearful recitation of how life is mistreating them and how no one cares for them. They play 'poor me' game with the victim. Beggars on Indian streets enact this very professionally.

f. **Guilt:** Manipulators take advantage of people who are willing to admit their own weaknesses by arousing a sense of guilt in them for displaying lack of cooperation with manipulators dictates. Manipulators will also highlight past sins to keep others in a state of guilt and shame.

How to avoid being manipulated:

No one likes to be manipulated, yet everyone at some time or the other would experience the phenomena of being manipulated much against their wishes. Having understood the general techniques a manipulator uses to achieve his objectives it becomes that much easier to avoid becoming a victim of manipulation. Some of the techniques to avoid being manipulated are listed below:-

a. **Avoid the manipulator:** Always get away from him or her. In fact, ignore them. If you cannot avoid the manipulator then give a blank stare rather than a spirited defense. It renders the manipulator ineffective. Nasty or intrusive communication does not require a response. Some psychologists believe that a narcissistic manipulator seeks any type of emotional response from others. It does not matter whether the response is positive or negative.

b. **Restate:** Ask the person to repeat or restate what he has just said. This a noble technique used in counseling. Firstly it gives you time to analyze what is being said and formulate a response and secondly the manipulator is likely to either change the statement or soften the stand.

c. **Talk straight:** Ask the manipulator to come to the point. This way he is exposed.

d. **Learn to say No:** Draw your boundaries and do not cross them under any pressure. Calmly but firmly say No.

e. **Do not stoop to his level:** Do not try to belittle him or bully him. Maintain your integrity and when necessary, disengage and walk away

Relevance to Study

Manipulation is of two types. Positive manipulation enhances the performance of the individual or group whereas negative manipulation is destructive in nature. Though manipulation as a subject and word generates negative feeling, its effects are not all negative. Positive manipulation is a motivating factor for higher and quality output. It therefore creates large life space. From the study it emerges that manipulation has positive correlation only with tact super rich and to a lesser degree with politician. There is reasonably amount of negative correlation with friends. With others it is negligible and not of much relevance. This goes to prove that in creating life space super rich and politicians are great manipulators while friends are poor manipulators of life space as compared to others. Also as per the correlation of manipulation with celebrities it emerges that there is a positive correlation with Lalu Prasad Yadav and to a lesser level with Smt

Indira Gandhi. The weakest correlation is with Dr Homi Bhaba and Swami Vivekanada. This reflects that amongst the celebrities Shri Lalu Prasad Yadav and Smt Indira Gandhi both politicians emerge as manipulators while Dr Homi Bhaba and Swami Vivekananda emerge as the weakest or non manipulators. This actually supplements our earlier finding that politicians are greater manipulators. Those who do not manipulate others create a larger life space. Amongst the manipulators only those who employ positive manipulation techniques create life space while those who employ negative techniques do not create any lasting life space.

Chapter 19

Charisma

Every human being desires recognition and seeks company of followers who will obey the individual's diktat. This is a difficult task and does not come easily to everybody. This desire is to be popular and to be center of attraction of a huge mass is driven by lot of parameters and constraints, which mostly are dependent on our personality and charisma. There are only a few who are gifted with such rare magnetic charisma; that human beings are drawn towards them like a bee towards honey, and willingly follow them. The study, recognition, and development of charisma in individuals are of particular interest to behavioural scientists, sociologists, psychologists and theologist to carry out research on the subject. In addition it has become a subject of special interest to public figures and celebrities like politicians, public speakers, actors, movie stars, music stars and upper echelons of social and business community.

Max Weber(1922) a sociologist of repute is the first person to empirically research this subject of charisma. Weber saw charismatic authority not so much as character traits of the charismatic leader but as a relationship between the leader and his followers .There is a similarity in the way Freud presented Gustave Le Bon's crowd psychology as the notion of identification and of an Ideal of the ego.

In politics, charismatic rule is often found in various dictatorship, authoritarian regimes and theocracies. In order to help to maintain their charismatic authority, such regimes generally rely on personality cult; which can be seen as an attempt to gain legitimacy by an appeal to other forms of authority. Weber mentions that when such a leader dies or leaves office and a new charismatic leader does not appear, such a regime is likely to fall; unless it has become fully routineised. Routineisation is the process by which 'charismatic authority is succeeded by a bureaucracy controlled by a rationally established authority or by a combination of traditional and bureaucratic authority' (Turner, Beeghley, and Powers, 1995 cited in Kendal et al. 2000). In "Economy and Society", (University of California Press 1985 [1922]), Max Weber distinguished between traditional, rational-legal, and charismatic modes of authority.

Innovated in sociology by Max Weber, the idea of charisma or charismatic authority is becoming increasingly important to the sociology of religion as well. Buddha, Mahavira, Mohammad, Jesus and other religious entities are considered charismatic as there are very few people that can be charismatic enough as to be remembered for more than thousands of years after their death.

In Weber's view, blindly following the charismatic leader tends to point to an irrational element in the behaviour of the follower. Charisma is therefore unusual, spontaneous, and creative of new movements and new structures. Being a source of instability and innovation charisma is a force for social change. Although vested in actual persons, charismatic leadership conveys to beholders certain sacred qualities, and followers respond by recognizing that it is their duty to serve the leader. Charisma is alien to the established institutions of society. Charismatic phenomena are temporary and unstable. Weber further elaborates that for that reason, charismatic authority is often 'routinized' during the lifetime of the new leader, so that he or she will be succeeded either by a non charismatic leader or by bureaucracy.(Gordon Marshal, 1998).

Len Oakes (1998), an Australian psychologist wrote a dissertation on charisma. His views are quite contrary to Weber's. Weber emphasized the social dynamics of charisma while Oakes in contrast focuses on the psychological framework of personality. In his research he made eleven charismatic leaders take the psychometric test. His findings revealed them as a group quite ordinary. Following the psychoanalyst Hienz Kohut, Oakes observed that charismatic leaders exhibit traits of narcissism. The narcissistic personality is characterized by self-styled notions of grandeur and a drive to manipulate and control his/her life and that of others. These days most of the political leaders especially in India are endowed with this trait. According to Oakes charismatic individuals compensate for this narcissistic shame by assuming the role of a prophet. They become what Sarah Hamilton-Byrne calls "a legend in their own mind." Such individuals motivate others with a driving mission to resolve a social or spiritual crisis

He further argues that they display an extraordinary amount of energy, accompanied by an inner clarity unhindered by the anxieties and guilt that afflict more ordinary people.

Definition

Some people have magnetic personality that draws others to them. Such a personality is known as charismatic personality. Charisma is derived from the Greek word χάρισμα (kharisma), "gift" or "divine favour," from kharizesthai, "to favour," from kharis, "favour". The Greek word "Charis" is the name for the Graces, the three goddess' sisters and daughters of Zeus the king of Gods. They are Brightfulness, Joyfulness, and Bloom. They are the triple incarnation of grace and beauty. As the fertility goddesses, they "gave life its bloom." Literally, a gift from the Gods, charisma is often thought of as an elusive quality for a chosen few. In actuality, we all have at least a hint of charisma. Charisma is not just for extroverts; it's something we can all learn to cultivate.

So charisma is basically defined as a rare personal quality attributed to leaders who arouse fervent popular devotion and enthusiasm. It is also viewed as personal magnetism or charm. In Christianity, it is described as an extraordinary power, such as the ability to perform miracles, granted by the Holy Spirit. Wayne Parker a consultant and prolific writer in one of his article wrote that Dr. Tony Alessandra has defined charisma as "the ability to influence others positively by connecting with them physically, emotionally, and intellectually." He also quotes Harvard anthropologist Charles Lindholm's definition: "Charisma is, above all, a relationship, a mutual mingling of the inner selves of leader and follower."

Political Dictionary describes charisma as originally a term from Christian theology, meaning 'a favour specially given by God's grace', the word was appropriated by Weber to mean 'a certain quality of an individual personality by virtue of which he is set apart from ordinary men and treated as endowed with supernatural or exceptional powers or qualities'. The term was used to refer to the spellbinding power of Hitler over the German people. Weber further highlighted that charisma by its nature cannot be passed on. Science Dictionary   on the other hand describes it as an extraordinary power and appeal of personality; natural ability to inspire a large following. Political leaders such as Mahatma Gandhi, religious leaders such as Swami Vivekanada, and entertainment figures such as Raj

Kapoor have all been described as charismatic as they had extreme charm and a 'magnetic' quality of personality along with innate and powerfully sophisticated personal communicability and persuasiveness.

Developing Charisma

Charisma is a certain quality of an individual personality, by virtue of which the individual is set apart from ordinary people and treated as endowed with supernatural, superhuman, or at least specifically exceptional powers or qualities. The French call it *"je ne sais quoi,"* or "I know not what," but the fact is, we do have words for these attributes. Charisma, chutzpah, joie de vivre and grace are four such enviable dispositions that defy easy definition, even though they are easily recognizable in people we admire. Different though they are, charisma, chutzpah, exuberance and equanimity project a positive energy that radiates beyond the person who embodies it (Carlin Flora,2007). These as such are not accessible to the ordinary person, but are regarded as divine in origin or as exemplary, and on the basis of them the individual concerned is treated as a leader. Celebrities across the globe crave to develop charisma. Volumes have been written on how to develop a charismatic personality.

According to the British professor Wiseman charisma is half innate and half developed. Broadcaster and confidence tutor Jeremy Milnes says that although charisma can be learnt, it can't be faked. Wayne Parker a trainer, consultant and writer, also professes that charisma can be developed, as it not a genetic trait. He further mentions that much of the profession of coaching is based on the premise that effective leadership skills, including charisma, can be developed in people. Parker quotes that charisma can be developed by developing the three dimensions cited by Dr. Alessandra i.e physical, emotional and intellectual. as the main attributes of charisma. Development of these attributes is elaborated below:-

Physical: Improvement of following physical skills to enhance charisma is recommended:-

- Improving overall health and energy levels.

- Enhancing ability to look people in the eye

- Developing a firm yet non-bone-crushing handshake.

- Investing in a better tailored wardrobe and looks.

- Carrying oneself better by holding head erect.

- Learning to smile more

Emotional: Charismatic leaders are emotionally balanced and are able to connect with others with ease. They are able to read the various signs and language of emotion and are able to communicate the same. Following need consideration in developing the emotional content of one's personality.

- Enhancing oral communication skills, including persuasion and public speaking

- Enhancing ability to communicate effectively in writing

- Focusing more on others and less on self while communicating

- Enhancing listening skills.

- More knowledgeable and aware of kinesics.

- Work on being more positive and optimistic

- Improve interpersonal relationships with all.

Intellectual: Charismatic leaders engage the minds of their followers and raise their ideas and ideals above the mundane. They think deeply about things and communicate those ideas and thoughts in simple meaningful ways. To enhance intellectual prowess consider the following:-

- Reading widely and deeply.

- Teaching, for actual learning begins while teaching others.

- Continuing professional development

- Learning about human behaviour

- Develop a better vocabulary

- Develop a habit of research.

British Professor Richard Wiseman as mentioned earlier has written extensively on the subject. of development of charisma. According to him a charismatic person has three major attributes. First they feel emotions themselves quite strongly. Second they are able to induce them in others. Third they are impervious to the influences of other charismatic people. Similar views have also been shared by Jake (2005). Based on these attributes Wiseman suggests some under mentioned external dimensions of personality that can be developed :-

- **General:** Open body posture, hands away from face when talking, stand up straight, relax, hands apart with palms forwards or upwards

- **To an individual:** Let people know they matter and you enjoy being around them, develop a genuine smile, nod when they talk, briefly touch them on the upper arm, and maintain eye contact

- **To a group:** Be comfortable as leader, move around to appear enthusiastic, lean slightly forward and look at all parts of the group

- **Message:** Move beyond status quo and make a difference, be controversial, new, simple to understand, counter-intuitive

- **Speech:** Be clear, fluent, forceful and articulate, evoke imagery, and use an upbeat tempo, occasionally slow for tension or emphasis.

Joe Love CEO of JLM & Associates In the article, " How To Become a Charismatic Leader," mentions that Charisma is based on the Law of Attraction. This law states that you inevitably attract into your life people and circumstances that harmonize with your dominant thoughts. Human beings are like a living magnet constantly radiating thought waves. Thoughts, intensified by emotions, radiate as radio waves duly intensified by electrical impulses. These are picked up by anyone who is tuned into a similar wavelength. People, ideas, opportunities, resources, circumstances are then all attracted into your life. Similar views have been written in one of the blogs on Personality and Charisma. Here the author mentions about will power. According to him human being is a charged particle; the orientation is controlled by the human brain. The atomic charge flow and orientation in human body is called Sarbionetics. The will power is the method of orientations. Recently one experiment in Japan has proved that will power of human can influence the movement of water in a glass. Similarly one man can also influence others. The author takes the example of Swami Vivekananda who once said (*"Ami gonduse somudra pan koribo, amar iccha matro porbot churno hoiya jaibe"*), that he can drink the whole sea in his hands, he can demolish mountain by virtue of his will power. Though being a simple monk, he had a phenomenal concentration and will power. More we have better we can control the action of the external world. One can increase ones will power through controlled and continuous practice of meditation, contemplation, believing and thinking of a particular subject or higher purpose or objective , which leads to some action. This power provides us huge determination and confidence, which enables us to form a charismatic and magnetic personality.

Joe Love (2005) further elaborates that the foundation for developing charisma is having a strong purpose. Individuals must seek a higher purpose and remain focused on accomplishing the great purpose. Lord Krishna at the end of the Great War sermons Arjuna on the relevance of purpose of existence and highlights that everything in this universe is created for a purpose and when its purpose is achieved it loses its relevance and therefore ceases to exist. (Kamala Subramaniam, 2004). Joe Love emphasizes development of strong self-confidence. This can be done by having intense belief in oneself. This belief is generated by developing requisite expertise or competence. People respect and admire the more knowledgeable in their field. Also charismatic persons take charge of situations therefore one must learn to take initiative and responsibility for our environment. Lastly he suggests looking inwards, work on the weaknesses and become deeply committed to development of positive attitude and character. (Joe Love,2005).

People with positive charismatic personality are observed to have spiritual inclination. All religious leaders like Jesus Christ, Prophet Mohammad, Lord Buddha, Guru Nanak Dev have all been spiritually charismatic. In Christianity it is believed that spiritual charisma can be developed by acquiring the under mentioned knowledge and qualities.

a. **Knowledge That Comes From Natural Intelligence:**
   Everyone has natural intelligence. This trait is closely associated to one's IQ. High intellectual ability is a gift from God. People gifted with this type of knowledge include Daniel (Dan. 6:1-4), Solomon (1 Kings 3:10-12), and Paul (2 Pet. 3:16-17).

b. **Knowledge That Comes From Active Christian Discipleship:**
   This can be developed by leading a sanctified life as per the teachings of Jesus Christ. A true disciple acquires spiritual knowledge and understanding that is divine in nature (1 Cor. 2:6-7).

c. **Knowledge That Comes From Personal Revelation:** Practitioners of spirituality receive personal revelation from the Divine for the benefit of the one receiving it, and may or may not be shared with other people. Examples of this kind of knowledge in the Bible includes Paul (2 Cor. 12:2-6), Peter and Cornelius (Acts 10:1-27), and James (Acts 15:13-20). One must practice spirituality in right earnest.

d. **Knowledge That Comes From Spiritual Charisma:** It is strongly believed that every Christian who is baptized in the Holy Spirit can receive divine revelation of Christ. This type of knowledge is temporary, immediate and completely the result of the Holy Spirit's presence. Its purpose is not to make someone a wise or knowledgeable person. As with other *spiritual charisma*, this knowledge is not for the benefit of the person receiving them, but is given for worldly benefit. Examples of this in the Bible includes Peter (Acts 5:1-4), Stephen (Acts 6:10), Ananias (Acts 9:10-12), and Paul (Acts 27:10-15). This form of divine revelation and knowledge can be acquired from true love, dedication and surrender to Lord Jesus Christ.

Similarly the fundamental doctrines of Buddhism preach: the Four Noble Truths, the Noble Eightfold Path, the Three Marks of Conditioned Existence, or Conditioned Co-production (*pa.ticca-samuppaada*) for attainment of moksha. The practioner of these doctrines is an illumined spiritual charismatic personality; the true Brahman. According to Buddha one becomes a Brahman or a non Brahman not by birth but by action. It is by austerity, by the holy life, by self-restraint, and self-taming, that one becomes a Brahman. Such a spiritual charisma of an enlightened soul can be developed by observing the following:-

a. **Renunciation (*pabbajjaa*):**   The lowest level of renunciation is simply that of material possessions. However, the practice is elevated to a much higher level than this. Attachment of any kind - whether material or mental - is viewed as an obstacle to realisation. The positive counterpart to this process of renunciation is the experience of contentment (*santushti)*.

b. **Independence or Solitariness (*Eka*):** A practitioners independence is his ability to withstand the 'worldly conditions' (*lokadhamma*): Solitude offers the aspirant a context in which to disentangle himself from the diluting and confusing bustle of the world and its narrow concerns and values and to strengthen his reserves of self-reliance.

c. **Non-violence (*ahimsa*) and Universal Loving-Kindness (*mettaa*):** It entails renunciation of all violence whether physical, verbal, or emotional feelings. These demands abandoning a host of negative mental states such as ill-temper, fury, grudge, rancour/ enmity or hostility, envy, violent destructiveness, malicious rage, or hatred.

d. **Humility/Modesty:** Humility is an important spiritual quality developed through self-confidence and dignity. A natural consequence of true humility is reverence, awe - and gratitude.

e. **Uprightness:** Involves being straightforward in dealings with other people. It also involves being free from deceit or duplicity of any kind.

f. **Calmness:** Effort should be made to still and calm the mind. This is developed by 'pacified senses' (*santindriya*); not at the mercy of instinctual urges and desires. An individual must discipline and focus his sense faculties - to 'guard the gates of the senses' - in accordance with his spiritual inclinations. Then a person transcends to calmness.

g. **Creative (*vigatakhila*):** The *Sutta-Nipaata* makes important use of an idiomatic Pali phrase, *vigatakhila*, to describe the flavour of the beatified sensibility. *Vigata* is 'gone away or 'ceased'. On a literal level, the *khila* is the land that is barren and yields no crops Buddha suggests that the true wasteland is within; it is one's own mind when not in a creative state. According to Buddhist philosophy one must develop a creative mind as it is profoundly optimistic. It generates love where there is no reason to love, develops an environment of happiness where there is no reason for happiness, creates where there is no possibility of creativity, and in this way 'builds a heaven in hell's despair. People with positive attitude are more creative.

h. **Good- words (*Subhaasita*):** In the Kokaalikasutta (sutta 3.10), the Buddha proclaims: One should speak what is righteous, not unrighteous. One should speak what is pleasant, not unpleasant. One should speak what is true, not untrue. One must only speak what he believes will be of benefit to others

Relevance to Life Space Management

Charismatic personality by its own grace creates a large life space. Normal man is not endowed with this trait. He does not experience the company of real charismatic personalities in his daily life as charismatic personalities in real sense are rare phenomena.

The surveyed population feels that charisma creates less space as compared to other factors. It is ranked very low also as the quantum of space it creates is also very less in terms of percentage. The reason for such assessment can be attributed to poor understanding of the term charisma, or poor experience of a charismatic personality. The results are further strengthened by poor correlation of charisma with other aspects of life space under consideration. From the surveyed results it is found to have a very weak and negligible correlation with other aspects of life space. The only viable correlation between charisma and various types of people is with super rich only; It is least with a politician. In so far as the celebrities are concerned the correlation is comparatively strongest with Aishwarya Rai &, Madhubala both film actors. It emerges that the surveyed population is more enamoured with the glamour and super rich rather than with others. Despite the fact that the population is attracted by these glamorous celebrities they do not create very large space with them. Lasting life space is still created by dynamic spiritual, intellectual and political leadership; as is evident from the following results:-

CELEBRITIES	LIFE SPACE CREATED IN %	RANKING
Swami Vivekanand	46.30%	1
Dr Homi bhaba	37.40%	2
Indira Gandhi	35.95%	3
Sai Baba	33.94%	4
Azmi Premji	31.95%	5
Sachin Tendulkar	34.40%	6
Dhyan Chand	31.23%	7
Aishwarya rai	27.29%	8
Madhubala	23.55%	9
Lalu Prasad Yadav	16.80%	10

Table 2 Life space created by various celebrities

Overall it emerges that Indian population is infatuated towards materialism like any normal human being. This infatuation might be the result of daily media blitz which the modern man is subjected to. Real charisma can only be experienced by coming in direct contact with the charismatic personality. Charismatic personalities need no make up to look attractive. It is only those who present a virtual personality that have to bank on external beautification of their persona. *Maya* thus emerges as more alluring. But *maya* being illusionary is short lived and temporary. Real positive charisma is one that endures. Charisma of spiritual masters has endured since times immemorial and therefore is a charisma that creates an everlasting life space. Life space created by great religious masters like Lord Jesus Christ, Lord Buddha, Lord Rama, Lord Krishna, Mohammad the Prophet, Lord Guru Nanak Dev, Sai Baba, Ram Krishan Paramhans, Swami Vivekananda etc is indelible, self sustaining and enduring. While life space created by the super rich Bill Gates, Ambanis, Tatas, or film actors will fade away on their demise or loss of wealth. As per Sri Aurobindo(1998) normal average mankind dwells in mind limited by looking towards life and body ; superior mankind levitates upwards towards truth of existence; supreme mankind further goes upwards to *Sat* and *Parabrahmana* or remains to beatify its lower members and raise to divinity in itself and others during their human existence. Despite all the allurements of Maya or materialism Indian mind is not polluted and remains alive to the relevance of everlasting charisma created by spiritual and intellectually inclined dynamic personalities.

Spiritual charisma can only be developed by spiritual practices. In India sages did tapas or meditation in solitude for very long periods and only then became enlightened and self realized souls. For common man of the world tapas may not be possible due to various human commitments essential for existence; however time can always be found for self improvement, meditation and spiritual existence.

Chapter 20

Life Space Creators at Domestic and Work Environment

Domestic Environment

We spend majority of our time either in domestic environment or at our workplace. In both the places we interact with people and create our relevance in their lives by creating the right amount of life space. Our entire relationship depends on how well we create the life space. At the domestic environment we come in contact with our parents, spouses, children and friends. A study of these four main characters reveals that the parameters of life space creators are different for different relations. The respondents were tasked to write three means adopted by them in creating life space with parents, spouses, children and friends. The results of survey are enumerated below:-

a. **Parents:** Here parents also reflect parental figures and elders of the family like grandparents, uncles and aunts. The results of the top 15 means of creating space with parents as per survey are as given below:-

Parents Score Card	
Item	score
Respect	119
Communication	105
Caring	105
Values	80
Love/affection	58
Self control	48

Parents Score Card	
Item	**score**
Character	48
Understanding	23
Help	23
Positive attitude	21
Obedience	18
Spend time	16
Tact	14
Sharing	12
Advise	12

Table 7 - Top 15 Responses: with parents

From the above data it emerges that the means of creating space with our parents are respect, communication, caring, values, love and affection, self control/ management character, understanding, help, positive attitude, obedience, spend time with them, tact, sharing and seek their advise in that order. An analysis of the data indicates that communication of a respectful loving and caring positive attitude towards the parents creates sound life space with parents. This attitude should be backed by sound values and character imbibed from them and the individual should be able to obey, share and give time to the parents. In Indian context respect for parental figures emerges as the strongest means of creating life space.

b.   **Spouse:** The results of the top 15 means of creating space with spouse as per survey are given below:-

(a) Spouse combined	
<u>Item</u>	**<u>Score</u>**
Communication	127
Love	89
Faith	48
Understanding	47
Respect	43

Positive attitude	35
Values	34
Character	33
Care	30
Sharing	29
Self Control	26
Tact	20
co-operation	18
Adjustment	11
Friend	10

Table 8 - Top 15 Responses: with spouse

From the above results it emerges that communication emerges as the most favoured means of creating life space. The above results display that spouses should communicate love, faith, understanding, respect, positive attitude, values, character, care, sharing, self control, tact, cooperation, adjustment and be friendly in that order. Communication of love, faith, understanding and respect are very essential for creating a large life space with the spouse.

c.   **Children:** The results of the top 15 means of creating space with children as per survey are as given below:-

(b) Children Combined	
Item	**Score**
Affection/love	138
values	105
communication	99
care	81
advice/guidance	47
character	41
understanding	26
Self control	24

friend	24
tact	23
attitude	20
playing	13
personality	13
giving time	11
encouragement	9

Table 9 - Top 15 Responses: with children

From the results affection/ love for the children emerges as the major creator of space with the children followed by values, communication , care, guidance, character, understanding in that order as shown above. The children are hungry for love and respect parents with values and character, who are understanding, caring and in times of crises give sound advice or guidance.

    d. Others (Friends and social circle): The results of the top 15 means of creating space with others in our social circle as per survey are as given below:-

Friends	
Item	**score**
communication	131
character	57
help	55
Positive attitude	50
values	36
personality	35
respect	27
Understanding	26
tact	26
sharing	21
Faith	21

affection/love	16
co-operation	15
charisma	15
care	14

Table 10 - Top 15 Responses: with friends.

The results reveal that the means of creating life space with others in our social environment are communication followed by character, help, positive attitude, values, personality, understanding, tact, sharing, faith, affection/ love, co-operation, charisma and care in that order. An analysis of the results reveals that the greatest and effective means of creating life space in our social circle can be achieved by developing sound and open communication means with the others in the environment. This should be supplemented by display of a personality with good character, values and positive attitude who is respectful, caring and has faith in others. The individual is also knowledgeable and is ever willing to extend love, help and share joys and sorrows with others.

e.   **Overall:** The results of the top 15 means of creating space with any one in our social circle as per survey are as given below:-

Total	
Item	**Score**
communication	462
love/affection	301
values	255
care	230
respect	195
character	179
Positive attitude	126
understanding	122
self control	110
help	96
tact	83

faith/trust	81
sharing	65
personality	60
advice/guidance	59

Table 11 - Summary of overall top 15 responses

From the above mentioned data it emerges that at individual level the skill and qualities that are required for creating life space are sound communication skills and a personality that has strength of character with sound values. Individual is able to extend and shower love and affection to one and all and has a caring, helpful and positive attitude. The individual is in control of the self; is trust worthy, tactful, very understanding and willing to share.

Creation of Life Space at Work Place:

The respondents were tasked to write three means adopted by them in creating life space with the Boss, Peers and Subordinates. The details of results obtained are listed below:-

a. **Boss:** Fifteen most common means of creating space with the boss as given out by respondents are shown below:-

MEANS	COMBINED SCORES
Communication	164
Positive attitude	68
Obedience	54
Respect	45
Work culture	32
Tact	31
Hard work	27
Sincerity	24
Values	20
Honesty	19
Understanding	18

Self control	18
Effective leadership	18
Character	16
Effective management	14

Table 12- Top 15 responses with boss

From the results it emerges that communication is the most favoured means of creating space with the boss. This is followed by display of positive attitude, obedience, respect, creation of sound work culture, tact, hard work, sincerity, values, honesty, understanding, self control/ management, effective leadership, character and effective management in that order. For creating large space with the boss we must remember to communicate a positive attitude, be obedient and respectful towards him/her. In addition display of hard work sincerity, tact and values would help.

b.   **Peers:** Fifteen most common means of creating space with the peers as given out by respondents are shown below:-

MEANS	COMBINED
Communication	129
Guidance / help	49
Values	48
Work culture	38
Friendliness	37
Positive attitude	36
Character	31
Understanding	27
Personality	27
Cooperation	27
Respect	26
Sself control	25
Sharing	20
Decision Making	18
Effective management	17

Table 13 - Top 15 responses: peers

From the data shown above it emerges that communication emerges as the main means of creating space with the peers in the organization. This is followed by guidance/ helping nature, sound values, good work culture, friendship, positive attitude, character, understanding, personality, cooperation, respect, self control/ management, sharing, decision making and effective management in that order. With the peers we must always keep the lines of communication open and display altruistic behaviour for creating a large life space.

c. **Subordinates:** Fifteen most common means of creating space with the subordinates as given out by respondents are shown below:-

MEANS	COMBINED
Communication	139
Effective leadership	50
Help	49
Work culture	34
Positive attitude	33
Tact	32
Values	30
Character	30
Employee satisfaction	26
Personality	20
Decision Making	20
Welfare	19
Respect	18
Friendly	17
Encouragement	17

Table 14 - Top 15 responses: subordinates

From the data shown above it emerges that communication emerges as the main means of creating space with the subordinates in the organization. This is followed by helping attitude, effective leadership, work culture, positive attitude, tact, values , character, employee satisfaction personality, decision making, welfare, respect, friendly, and encouragement in that order. With the subordinates a leader must display effective leadership qualities that is caring and helpful has the ability to create the right working environment and is possessing positive attitude and has sound values, for creating a large amount of space.

d. Overall: Fifteen most common means of creating space in an organisation as given out by respondents are shown below:-

<u>**Overall**</u>	<u>**Score**</u>
Communication	432
Positive attitude	137
Help	113
Work culture	104
Values	98
Respect	89
Tact	79
Character	77
Effective leadership	72
Friendly	59
Personality	56
Understanding	55
Obedience	54
Self control	53
Decision Making	49

Table 15 - Overall top 15 responses

From the above data it emerges that in an organizational context sound communication emerges as the main means of creating life space with others. This is followed by positive attitude helping nature, good work culture, values, respect, tact, character, effective leadership, friendly, personality, understanding, obedient, self control/ management and sound decision making in that order. Obedience is only applicable in creating space with the boss as per the respondents while the other chosen parameters are applicable to all.

Chapter 21

Creation of Life Space at Organisational Level

Organizations are created to meet the felt need of the environment. Organizations consist of people and are a sound mechanism for them to coexist for attainment of set out goals. (Mishra & Mathur, 1997). These goals can be achieved if proper management techniques are employed. Lot of study has been undertaken to study how organizations are created and how they function effectively to achieve their set out objectives.   Further any organisation that is not effective will soon fade away. All organizations work hard to remain relevant in the environment. This relevance is created by creating the right amount of life space. If the organization is not able to create life space with its stakeholders then the organization will decay and soon cease to exist. Organisations must therefore learn to manage their life space and master this art to remain relevant and effective in the environment that they exist in.

This chapter analyses data collected from respondents on the parameters that create life space at the organizational level. Data was also collected from the respondents about the concept of Life space management from the parameters of life space management that are applicable at the organizational level. Parameters were given to the respondents based on the expert opinion and focused group discussion. The respondents were asked to give their opinion whether the given parameters create life space or not and also state their effectiveness.

From the data analyzed for finding out the percentage of respondents who answered in affirmative that the given parameters create life space at organizational level; the outcome of the analysis is as shown below:-

Parameters	Percentage
Effective Management Team	80.32%
Work culture	78.64%
Effective Leadership	77.10%
Employee satisfaction	75.16%
Org Ethics	74.51%
Decision Making	74.51%
Good public relations	73.23%
Communication	73.23%
Stakeholders satisfaction	57.74%
Power Projection	48.06%

Table 16 - Response of respondents in percentage

From the survey results it emerges that maximum respondents (approximately 80%) agree that effective management team creates life space at organizational level. This is followed by work culture, effective leadership, employee satisfaction, organizational ethics, decision making, good public relations, stake holders satisfaction and power projection in that order.

This is further substantiated by rank ordering the importance in which these parameters create life space at organizational level. This is as shown in the chart below:-

Parameters	COMBINED
Effective Management Team	1
Effective Leadership	2
Work culture	3
Decision Making	4
Employee satisfaction	5
Communication	6
Ethics	7
Good public relations	8
Stake holders satisfaction	9
Power projection	10

Table 17 Rank ordering of parameters of life space creators at organizational level

From the rank ordering it emerges that Effective Management team emerges as number one creator of life space followed by effective leadership, work culture, decision making, employee satisfaction, communication, ethics, good public relations, stake holder's satisfaction, and power projection.

To further understand the relevance of various parameters in creating life space at organizational level; a detailed understanding of each parameter is a must. These are elaborated in subsequent chapters

Chapter 22

Effective Management Team

Effective management team has been rated as the single largest life space creator at organizational level. If the management team is good the organization will prosper and grow while if the management team is ineffective the organization is certainly going to suffer. It is for this reason good and effective managers come at a price. It is also observed that large corporate houses are willing to foot the bill to get the best on board of their companies.

"Management team" is part of a formal leadership structure of an organization usually consisting of a group of managers who report to the same boss. They have common organizational goals. They meet regularly to share information and make decisions that affect the whole organization or department for which they are responsible. Team leadership and membership is dependent on the positions individuals hold in the organizations. Effective management team is the creation of the leadership. Effective management team also reflects good work culture and conducive work environment.

Relevance to the study

Effective management team has emerged as the most favoured factor of creating life space in organisations. Maximum respondents 80.32% have endorsed it as one of the major factor in creating life space. Respondents are also of the opinion that effectiveness of an effective management team in creating life space with others is 48.04%, which is substantially large.

It is also observed that effective management team has a positive and strong correlation with work culture and employee satisfaction in that order. This implies that a good work culture and corresponding employee satisfaction are an outcome of the efforts of effective management team. The correlation of effective management team is as given in the succeeding table shown below:-

	Eff Mgt Team	**Work Culture**	**Employee Satisfaction**
Pearson Correlation	1	0.423591	0.284011
Sig. (2-tailed)	.	6.28E-15	3.67E-07
Sum of Squares and Cross-products	2057.084	901.7935	620.9935
Covariance	6.657229	2.918426	2.009688
N	310	310	310

Table 18 - Relevant correlation of effective management team at organizational level

This confirms the findings of other researches on the importance of an effective management team in an organization. All organizations are therefore always on the lookout for hiring the best managers to enhance their organizational effectiveness.

Chapter 23

Effective Leadership

Difference between an effective and non effective organization is the difference between the leadership provided in both organizations. An organization can rise from ruins to scale the highest pinnacles of success and vice versa based on the leadership provided to that organization. Such is the impact of a good or bad leadership. It is for this reason the respondents have given importance to effective leadership as the means of creating large life space for an organization. Effective leaders will create effective management teams and effective management teams will create large life space for the organization in the environment.

Relevance to the Study

Effective leadership is the backbone of effective organizations. The table given below reveals the relevant correlation between effective leadership and other parameters of Life Space. From the data obtained from our study it emerges that effective leadership has a positive correlation with communication followed with decision making and ethics. It implies that effective leaders are good communicators, good decision makers with sound ethical practices or sound values. Based on these they create good work culture, create effective management teams that enhance employee satisfaction. The details of relevant correlation of effective leadership with other parameters are as given below:-

	Effective Leadership	Communication	Decision Making	Ethics
Pearson Correlation	1	0.299522	0.289253	0.114785
Sig. (2-tailed)	.	7.61E-08	2.18E-07	0.043433
Sum of Squares and Cross-products	2144.194	757.7742	549.2903	264.129
Covariance	6.939138	2.452344	1.777639	0.854787
N	310	310	310	310

Table 19 - Relevant correlation of effective leadership at organizational level

Among the respondents 77.10 % agree that effective leadership is responsible for creating the right life space for organizations. However in so far as the quantum of life space is concerned it is observed that effective leadership creates the largest amongst all parameters. It creates up to 49. 60 % life space while effective management creates 48.04 %. Defence personnel give greater credence to leadership in creating life space as compared to civilians. As per defence personnel effective leadership can create up to 55. 82 % of life space for an organization while civilians attribute only 37.53 %. This difference in opinion also may be the result of wieghtage Defence Forces give to their leadership and its relevance to their profession. In industry especially at one time there was a raging debate whether industry needed good leaders or good managers. Now that problem is resolved and everyone agrees on the necessity and supremacy of leadership. Leadership is the main catalyst in creating a huge life space by the organizations in the environment.

Chapter 24

Work Culture

In this age of globalization and opening up of our economy, Indian Industry is progressing by leaps and bounds. Foreign investors are lining up to open shop in India. Everyone is keen to learn about Indian work culture and work ethos. Otherwise too it is essential to learn of the culture of an organization in order to facilitate dealing with the organization more effectively. Edgar Schein, who has written extensively on various facets of culture and its impact on organizations supplements the necessity of learning about the culture of own organization. He mentions "The bottom line for leaders is that if they do not become conscious of the cultures in which they are embedded, those cultures will manage them."

Relevance to Study

Working environment in any organization is dependent on work and organizational culture of the organization. It is observed that effective organizations have positive work culture. Positive work culture develops positive outlook in the employees. Conversely positive work culture is developed by employees having positive outlook and attitude. Pritam Kaur (May 2004) too advocates that organizations must develop positive culture to enhance their growth and reputation. An organization cannot meet its objectives unless positive work culture exists. Poor and unhygienic working conditions, stagnation, lack of appreciation / incentives and rewards, all add up to kill employee's creativity and interest. Positive work culture not only develops an organization, it provides satisfaction to its personnel. 78.64% respondents agree that work culture does create large life space in an organization. Work culture has been ranked as number 3 factor in an organization that creates maximum life space after effective management team & effective leadership. Work culture has a very strong and positive correlation with effective management team and employee satisfaction. The details are as given below:-

	Work Culture	Eff Mgt Team	Employee Satisfaction
Pearson Correlation	1	0.423591	0.344906
Sig. (2-tailed)	.	6.28E-15	4.36E-10
Sum of Squares and Cross-products	2203.277	901.7935	780.4774
Covariance	7.130348	2.918426	2.525817
N	310	310	310

Table 20 - Relevant correlation of work culture at organizational level

Respondents also feel that good positive work culture can create up to 45.32% of life space for an organization. This confirms that sound and positive work culture is essential for enhancing the effectiveness of an organization.

Chapter 25

Decision Making

Humans are endowed with the element of choice. In a given situation individuals behave and react differently based on their decision in choosing between several options. All actions are an outcome of this decision making ability of the individual. At organizational level all planning and actions are also subject to decision making ability of its management. Decision making itself is a complex phenomenon and has been a subject of active research from several perspectives. From psychological perspective, individual decisions can be examined in the context of individual preferences, a set of needs, emotions, and values individual seeks. From a cognitive perspective, the decision making process must be regarded as a continuous process integrated in the interaction with the environment .From a normative perspective, the analysis of individual decisions is concerned with the logic of decision making and rationality and the invariant choice it leads to. .

Signs of good leadership are the ability to lead effectively. To lead effectively, requires the ability to make good decisions. Effective leaders learn to do this in a timely and well-considered way. They are thus able to lead their team to spectacular and well-deserved success. Ineffective leaders are observed to dither or make poor decisions; thus their teams or organizations risk and suffer from failure. Decision making creates stress in the decision maker as all decisions have an element of future involved in them. Future is an unknown area and therefore a stress creator. Subordinates respect the management that is quick in taking decisions and abhor bureaucratic delays.

There are several kinds of decisions. They can be classified based on timelines or on types of alternatives generated:-

a.   **Whether this or that:** This is between two choices or alternatives and generally taken as yes / no, either /or. Such decisions are made by weighing reasons pro and con.

b.   **Which One:** These decisions involve a choice of one or more alternatives from among a set of possibilities, the choice being based on how well each alternative measures up to a set of predefined criteria.

c.   **Contingent decisions:** These are decisions that have been made but put on hold until some condition is met.

d.   **Short Term:** Decisions that have short term effect. These are routine in nature and can also be called operational decisions.

e.   **Mid Term:** Decisions that have midterm impact. These can also be called Tactical decisions.

f.   **Long Term:** Decisions that have a long term impact. These can also be called as Strategic Decisions.

As every decision is made within a decision environment, every decision is thus affected by the environment and the ability of the decision maker to read the environment. This decision environment provides information, alternatives, values, and preferences. An ideal decision environment would include all possible information, all of it accurate, and every possible alternative. However, both information and alternatives are constrained because time and effort to gain information or identify alternatives is an expensive business. Based on the environment some of the decisions are thus a mix of the above mentioned categories. Also with passage of time the environment keeps expanding; more information is available. This may lead to decision maker delaying taking a decision till the critical stage is reached. Sometimes many decision makers develop a tendency to seek more information than required to make a good decision. When too much information is sought and obtained, several problems crop up like as given below:-

a.   A delay in the decision occurs; which could impair the effectiveness of the decision or solution.

b.   Information overload will occur.

c. Selective use of the information will occur. That is, the decision maker will choose from among all the information available only those facts which support a preconceived solution or position.

d. Mental fatigue occurs, which results in slower work or poor quality work.

e. Decision fatigue occurs, where the decision maker tires of making decisions. Often the result is fast, careless decisions or even decision paralysis--no decisions are made at all.

Everyone is concerned with the quality of the decision as it impinges on individual and organizational effectiveness. In judging the quality of a decision, in addition to the concerns of logic, use of information and alternatives, three other considerations come into play as shown below:-

(a) The decision must meet the desired objectives thoroughly and completely.

(b) The decision must meet the desired objectives efficiently and in cost effective manner.

(c) The decision must take into account the outcomes like valuable by products or indirect advantages.

(d) The decision should have acceptability. (Robert Harris, 1998).

Relevance to the Study

The process of **corporate decision making** is of the utmost importance for effective management. Some manager will be authoritative while others democratic in their decision making. The decision making process in both cases must be informed by expert knowledge and experience. (thinkingmanagers.com, Internet, May 08).Decision-making is more natural to certain personalities. Such people should focus more on improving the quality of their decisions. People who are less natural decision-makers are often able to make quality assessments, but then need to be more decisive in acting upon the assessments made.

Problem-solving and decision-making are closely linked, and each requires creativity in identifying and developing options. Thinking, out of the box technique, brainstorming, SWOT analysis, decision tree and other modern decision making tools are all very useful in improving the quality of decisions and must be extensively used by the managers. (businessballs. com, Internet, May 08).

Good decision making is a positive reflection of effective leadership, acts as good PR, reflects power, and ethics of the organisation. Correlation of decision making with other parameters is as shown in the chart given on the opposite page.

From the above table it emerges that decision making has a positive correlation with effective leadership followed by good PR, power projection, ethics and communication in that order. It is observed to have a negative correlation with employee satisfaction and work culture. It implies that certain decision may not at times be viewed positively by the employees. Poor decision making can lead to poor employee satisfaction which in turn over a period of time will negatively impact the work culture of the organization.

In our survey Decision Making has been ranked at number 4 amongst other parameters that create life space at organizational level. From the survey it is also observed that good decision making can be responsible for creating upto 48.45% of life space for the organization in the environment. Organisations must therefore pay greater attention to the decision making skills of their management and should also streamline the decision making process in the organisation.

	Decision Making	Eff Leadership	Good PR	Power Projection	Ethics	Communication	Work Culture	Employee Satisfaction
Pearson Correlation	1	0.289253	0.234545	0.206169	0.197354	0.142442	-0.11138	-0.17198
Sig. (2-tailed)	.	2.18E-07	3.03E-05	0.000258	0.000474	0.012051	0.050077	0.002378
Sum of Squares and Cross-products	1681.835	549.2903	426.4129	557.271	402.1935	319.1613	-214.413	-340.013
Covariance	5.442833	1.777639	1.379977	1.803466	1.301597	1.032884	-0.69389	-1.10037
N	310	310	310	310	310	310	310	310

Table 21 - Relevant correlation of decision making at organizational level

Chapter 26

Employee Satisfaction

For decades organizations have paid attention to people and have said that they are the most important part of the organization. (CR Grindle, 1969). Research shows that satisfied and motivated employees facilitate higher production, greater customer satisfaction and, in turn, positively influence organizational performance and effectiveness. The link between employee attitude and customer satisfaction can be seen both in quantitative studies and in everyday life. Organizations that invest in measuring employee opinions and attitudes, by incorporating Employee Satisfaction Surveys into their existing HR processes, can develop such a workforce. A lot of research work has been done on motivation and enhancement of employee satisfaction.

Relevance to the study

From the survey as well study of literature it emerges that satisfied employees produce satisfied customers and satisfied customers help to grow any business. Only satisfied employees willingly make contributions to the organization to ensure its financial security and longevity. They also take pride in their organizations; their work and, feel valued. They welcome personal development and growth; feel free to share their opinions and ideas honestly; and better serve the needs of the stakeholders.

From the survey it is observed that greater importance is given to employee satisfaction by civilians as compared to defence personnel. This may be due to the inherent nature of soldiering wherein mission completion at all cost is given more weightage. Despite this approach, it is noticed that the military leaders are more concerned for the safety and welfare of their subordinates than their civilian counterparts. Therefore while quantifying the degree of effectiveness employee satisfaction creates in an organization it is observed that the defence personnel have given it more wieghtage as compared to civilians as is evident from the data shown in the chart given below:-

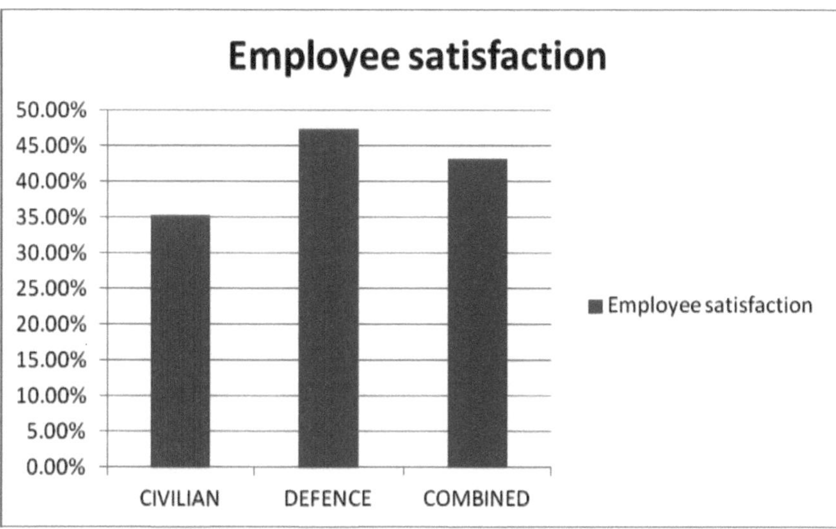

Chart 5.6 Life space created by employee satisfaction at organizational level

The correlation of employee satisfaction with other parameters is as given below:-

	Employee Satisfaction	Work Culture	Eff Mgt Team	Stake Holders Satisfaction	Good PR
Pearson Correlation	1	0.344906	0.284011	0.245402	0.16916
Sig. (2-tailed)	.	4.36E-10	3.67E-07	1.24E-05	0.002809
Sum of Squares and Cross-products	2324.077	780.4774	620.9935	665.1935	361.5226
Covariance	7.521286	2.525817	2.009688	2.15273	1.169976
N	310	310	310	310	310

Table 22 - Relevant correlation of employee satisfaction at organizational level

From the above data it emerges that employee satisfaction has a reasonably strong and positive correlation with work culture, followed by effective management team, stake holder satisfaction and good public relations in that order. This proves the point that satisfied employees create a very healthy work culture. Also a healthy work culture reflects high satisfaction of employees. Satisfied employees in turn create a very good life space for the organization. Therefore management must design strategies for enhancing employees' satisfaction.

Chapter 27

Organisational Communications

There can be no organization without people. People depend on organisations for their sustenance and living. People cannot interact with each other without communication. In the absence of communication, everything would grind to a halt. Communication thus becomes the life source of organisations because organisations involve people. The importance of communication in organisations is well established by the researchers, based on the amount of time spent by members on communicating in organisations. According to them, members in organisations spend 50 to 80 per cent of their time engaged in communicative behaviour.

Paul Turner in his article mentions that effective communication in the workplace is essential for the delivery of successful organizational strategy and change, employee commitment, and ultimately competitive advantage. It is observed that the ability to engage stakeholders through excellent communication strategy and action in an organization is now an essential competence required specially in the sales and marketing people. Without this competence the chance of the organization achieving its strategic objectives are reduced substantially. Corporate thus spend a lot on communicating with its stakeholders. Within companies too, we see the evolution of definite communication systems and processes, be it oral or written, through the combination of the available media viz: text, graphics, image, animation, audio or video. So its relevance has been accepted as an essential function of management to achieving success in any organization.

While effective communication brings success, the lack of it makes matters worse for organizations is an accepted fact. It does not matter which important person heads the organisation, if he is not able to show leadership through communication, we will eventually see a sick or disintegrating institution.

We need to understand the cardinal principle in communication and that is, communication is what is understood, not what is delivered. Often, people dwell on the fact that they have communicated enough but the end result shows otherwise. It is here one has to understand the flaws in the delivery of the communication, resulting in the receiver not grasping the essence of it. Be ready to course-correct and innovate the way communication is delivered.

Communication Strategies

Each organization designs and implements its own communication strategies to achieve success. For effective communication in specialized contexts like marketing etc, certain strategies can be taken that will help organisations achieve their goals and can be seen as techniques for attaining the purpose of communication. Since business is all about marketing of products and services some of the effective communication strategies used in marketing and selling are as given below:-

(a) **Continuous Innovation:** It is adopted by industry specially large enterprises. It requires building or improving products, services, and processes to enhance customer satisfaction.

(b) **Entrepreneurial Management:** Describes a business where the employees are expected to work and relate to each other as self driven business partners.

(c) **One Voice:** In this strategy one person is designated the leader and other team members direct all their comments and questions through the designated leader "One Voice speaker," to manage customer team meetings.

(d) **Show Time:** A term related to business people during a meeting or visit by a customer.

(e) **Strategic Speed:** A term related to working fast and smart, constantly looking for opportunities to improve and innovate.

(f) Discipline of Dialogue: A term related to controlling your words and conversations during a business meeting or presentation.

Relevance to Study

At individual level communication has been ranked higher as a parameter for creating life space than at organizational level. At organizational level it has been ranked at number 6. From the study it is also observed that communication has a positive correlation with effective leadership, followed by power projection, ethics, good PR, and decision making in that order. The details are as given in the chart given below:-

	Communication	Effective Leadership	Power Projection	Ethics	Good PR	Decision Making
Pearson Correlation	1	0.299522	0.296668	0.228547	0.161417	0.142442
Sig. (2-tailed)	.	7.61E-08	1.02E-07	4.87E-05	0.004382	0.012051
Sum of Squares and Cross-products	2985.097	757.7742	1068.323	620.5161	390.9677	319.1613
Covariance	9.660507	2.452344	3.457355	2.008143	1.265268	1.032884
N	310	310	310	310	310	310

<u>Table 23 - Relevant correlation of communication at organizational level</u>

From the above table it is amply evident that good leaders are also good communicators. From the survey it is also observed that a good and sound communication processes in an organization can create up to 45.95% of life space.

People cannot interact with each other without communication. Nair mentions that effective communication is the key to success as it leads to good relationship, trust and confidence, all of which are positive traits required for better living at individual level. As organizations consist of human beings similar analogy can be applied to organisations. While structuring or restructuring an organization decision centers should be identified and channel of communication so designed that it facilitates in decision making and communication of the decision to the implementers of those decision. Communication process is also fundamental to the change implementation process and perception building. All organizations attempt at building good perception of the organization through sound communication means. Effective leaders use sound organisation communication means and tools for creating good organisational life space in the environment.

Chapter 28

Organisation Ethics

Ethics is a very broad concept. In literature there are several definitions and interpretations of this concept. There are no universally agreed rules of ethics, no absolute standards or controls, and no fixed and firm reference points as ethics depends on the interpretation of the subject. Despite all forms of interpretation it is fascinating to observe that how important ethics have now become in modern life and society.

The American Heritage Dictionary of the English Language mentions that the word ethic has its origin in middle English ethik, from Old French ethique,from Late Latin ēthica, from Greek ēthika, ethics and from Latin ēthicē. It further defines ethics as the rule or standards governing the conduct of a person or the members of a profession. Thesaurus describes it as motivation based on ideas of right and wrong as also the philosophical study of moral values and rules. Wikipedia, the free encyclopedia defines ethics as a major branch of philosophy, encompassing right conduct and good life. It is significantly broader than the common conception of analyzing right and wrong. A central aspect of ethics is "the good life", the life worth living or life that is simply satisfying, which is held by many philosophers to be more important than moral conduct. Some of the philosophical ethical concepts that emerge are as given below:-

a. **Hedonism:** It believes that the principal ethic is maximizing pleasure and minimising pain. There are several schools of Hedonist thought ranging from those advocating the indulgence of even momentary desires to those teaching a pursuit of spiritual bliss. In their consideration of consequences, they range from those advocating self gratification regardless of the pain and expense to others, to those stating that the most ethical pursuit maximizes pleasure and happiness for the most people.

b. Stoicism: This philosophical school was founded by Zeno. It laid emphasis on control of passions. One of the great stoic philosopher Epicteus preached that the greatest good was contentment and peace of mind. Self-mastery over one's desires and emotions leads to spiritual peace. Freedom from material attachments and abstinence of sex and sexual desires is central to this philosophy. Stoic philosophy recommends accepting things that cannot be changed, resigning oneself to existence and enduring in a rational fashion. Epictetus said difficult problems in life should not be avoided, but rather embraced. Spiritual exercises are needed for the health of the spirit, just as physical exercise is required for the health of the body. Epictetus said remaining abstinent in the face of temptation was a victory for which a man could be proud.

c. Normative Ethics: Traditionally, normative ethics (also known as moral theory) was the study of what makes actions right and wrong. Normative ethic offers an overarching moral principle to which one could appeal in resolving difficult moral decisions.

d. Meta Ethics: Meta-ethics is concerned primarily with the meaning of ethical judgments and/or prescriptions and with the notion of which properties, if any, are responsible for the truth or validity thereof. Meta-ethics as a discipline gained attention with GE Moore's(1903) famous work Principia Ethica, in which Moore first addressed what he referred to as the naturalistic fallacy.

e. Descriptive ethics: Descriptive ethics examines ethics not from a top-down perspective but rather as observation of actual choices; made by moral agents in practice. Some philosophers rely on descriptive ethics and choices made and unchallenged by a society or culture as the basis to categories ethics.

f. Applied Ethics: Applied ethics is a discipline of philosophy that attempts to apply ethical theory to real-life situations. The lines of distinction between meta-ethics, normative ethics, and applied ethics are often blurred and overlapping.

Organisational ethics can be defined as the articulation, application and evaluation of the consistent values and moral positions of an organization by which it is identified, both internally and externally. It is also the responsibility of the top management to spell out the ethical practices of the organization and to ensure that they are carried out in letter and spirit. It is the responsibility of HR personnel to build and monitor ethical practices in any organization.

Many organisations these days emphasize on having formal ethical development programmes but they are of little use without strong role models that lead the way in creating an ethical culture. In defence forces this role is played by the military commander but in industry it is observed that HR professionals are best suited to act as ethical role models considering their immense sway on the entire workforce. Ethical conduct of employees largely depends on how they perceive the organisational policies. If the policies are viewed as ethical the employees are motivated to work ethically and if they perceive the policies as unfair they tend to adopt unethical behaviour. (Poornima Srikrishna, Internet, May 08). . Top managers play an important role in establishing its ethical tone. Managers who want employees to behave ethically must first exhibit ethical behaviour and decision making practices themselves. Managers have to remember that leading by example is the first step in fostering a culture of ethical behavior in their companies. No matter what the formal policies say or what they are told to do, if employees see managers behaving unethically, they will believe that the company wants them to act in a like manner. An ethical workforce enhances organizational effectiveness and vice-versa.

The sources of ethics are partly man's own experience and partly the principles and truths proposed by other philosophical disciplines. Ethics takes its origin from the empirical fact that certain general principles and concepts of the moral order are common to all people at all times. Different people however interpret these principles differently and have different beliefs about what constitutes ethical behavior. The law defines what is and is not legal, but the distinctions between moral right and wrong are not always so clear. In many situations lines between right and wrong are blurred. Such situations can lead to ethical dilemmas and thus differing views. In view of the chaos of opinions and systems just described, modern young managers seem to be influenced by hedonism and by Nietzsche, the originator of a school of thought whose doctrines are founded on the principle 'that alone is good which serves my interests.' Buisness done on these principles are short lived. In the end organizations based on sound values and ethical practices survive.

Relevance to the study

Modern culture which is the outcome of materialism is hedonistic and can be labeled as 'greedy'. We learn from the environment which we exist in. Despite the forces at work to bring in hedonistic ethics there is a growing awareness of its pitfalls and a move towards normative and applied ethics. It is amply evident as more and more organisations in the business world develop codes of ethics that they expect each member to follow. This paradigm for organisational ethics is largely concerned with extracting the best possible results for the organisation as a whole. When acting within a certain environment, be it local, national or global, the organisation wants to be seen to be 'socially acceptable' thus maintaining a good standing in the public eye.

As per study organizational ethics are found to have positive correlation with stake holders satisfaction, power projection, good PR, communication and effective leadership in that order. The details are as given below:-

	Ethics	Stake Holders Satisfaction	Power Projection	Communication	Good PR	Decision Making	Eff Leadership
Pearson Correlation	1	0.285278	0.283147	0.228547	0.254275	0.197354	0.114785
Sig. (2-tailed)	-	3.24E-07	3.99E-07	4.87E-05	5.8E-06	0.000474	0.043433
Sum of Squares and Cross-products	2469.419	797.0968	927.3871	620.5161	560.1613	402.1935	264.129
Covariance	7.991648	2.579601	3.001253	2.008143	1.81282	1.301597	0.854787
N	310	310	310	310	310	310	310

Table 24 - Relevant correlation of ethics at organizational level

As per the survey respondents feel that sound organization ethics can help create upto 39.40 % of life space for an organization. Organisations with sound ethical practices create a large life space with their stakeholders.

Chapter 29

Good Public Relations (PR)

Like Other parameters PR too does not have any single definition. One of the definition is ' relations with the general public through publicity; those functions of a corporation, organization, branch of military service, etc., concerned with informing the public of its activities, policies, etc., and attempting to create favourable public opinions'. Another dictionary describes it as actions taken to promote goodwill. (Cutlip & Center, 1982). In 1947 Public Relations News, one of the commercial news letter defined public relations as the management function which evaluates public attitudes, identifies the policies and procedures of an individual or organization with public interest and executes a program of action to earn public understanding and acceptance.

PR is extensively used by organizations including industry, the government and even celebrities especially prominent politicians during their campaigns before elections. All of them try to read public opinions and attempt to change that opinion /attitude to a favourable one through the mechanism of good PR. In short all of them attempt to create the right life space with their stake holders in the environment. It is for this reason that heavy amounts are spent on PR during US presidential elections. Now days even in India each political party establishes PR cell and teams and PR strategies and policies which are implemented during the elections or before implementation of certain rules regulations or policies by the government.

Historically PR is not new it was extensively used by the Greeks and subsequently by the Romans. Romans coined the expression *vox populi, vox Die,* meaning ' the voice of people is the voice of God.' In India too in ancient historical records there is a mention of king's spies whose function was beside espionage to keep the king in touch with public opinion and to market the king and his policies favourably in public. However the first recorded tool of PR was designed and used by Harvard College in 1643 when the first fund raising brochure was printed in London. (Cutlip & Centre, 1982)

There is a famous maxim for initiating PR; 'Any business must show its ability to succeed without public relations before public relations can do any good.' Management normally does not recognize PR unless money is spent on it. These days all organizations have a PR department. This department must be fully integrated with the rest of the organization to be effective in its task of changing public opinion favourably. (David Finn, 1960)

Good customer relations are the root of PR function in an industry .(Jefkins, 1987). PR professionals undertake surveys to obtain public opinion and thereafter design strategies to change the public opinion in favour of the organizations. All forms of media are generally used by the PR people. The tools normally used are as follows:-

(a) Interviews of Top Management

(b) Press Conferences.

(c) Press Release.

(d) Feature Articles.

(e) Reporting News Making Events

(f) Tie up with media.

(g) Dramatic features concerning the organization included in film or by an TV anchor.

(h) Social media. (Facebook, Twitter, Whatsaap etc.)

(i) Photographs

(j) Other publicity means.

Relevance to Study

The growth of PR in all government as well as industry is a clear indication of its relevance in creating life space for the concerned organizations in the environment. Indeed, there is considerable evidence that public relations can and does do well. Organisations such as the Red Cross would not have enough blood, charities would lack funds, and communities would be unaware of important government programs without public relations campaigns.

Jim R McNamara carried out a research on Impact of Media on PR . He carried out a survey of 417 journalists and editors in Sydney, Melbourne, Brisbane and Canberra, as part of a Masters Degree in 1992. He found 86% reported 'Very Frequent' contact from PR practitioners. More than 74% reported receiving 20 or more PR communications (news releases, phone calls, faxes, etc) per week. In the same period, 150 news releases from 27 different companies and organisations were obtained and content analysis was undertaken of the media in which the journalists were employed over a 12 months period. Articles were identified using a national press clipping service which provided 2,500 articles on the topics of the news releases from the selected media. The findings of the study observed the following:-

(a) 768 stories (31%) were wholly or partly based on the news releases (including exact extracts or facts and figures without alternative attribution). While 360 (47%) of these were published in trade or specialist media, 245 stories (32%) of PR-based stories were published in national, State or capital city media;

(b) Up to 70% of the content of some small trade, specialist and suburban media was PR-sourced;

(c) Only nine news releases out of 150 tracked (1.2%) were not used at all by the media;

(d) The average usage rate of news releases was seven times each;

(e) One news release (on a Lindeman Wines product) was published in 69 newspapers, many with a photograph provided by the PR firm.

From the study of responses of respondents it emerges that Good PR has a reasonably strong and positive correlation with stake holders satisfaction, followed by power projection, ethics, decision making, employee satisfaction and communication in that order. It is a powerful means for power projection. It is because of this that each nation and government spends billions of dollars on creating good PR. This is further substantiated by the fact that good PR also has a positive correlation with politician, King/Queen and actor in that order. These three categories extensively use PR to enhance their life space in the environment. The details of correlation of good PR with other parameters are as shown in Table 25 opposite.

From the the study of McNamara it is evident that even the media relies heavily on PR departments and organizations to publish their stories. From our own research it emerges that Good PR can create upto 38.55 % of life Space for an organization.

	Good PR	Stake Holders Satisfaction	Power Projection	Ethics	Decision Making	Employee Satisfaction	Communication	Politician	King/Queen	Actor
Pearson Correlation	1	0.395088	0.352178	0.254275	0.234545	0.16916	0.161417	0.185408	0.160217	0.158872
Sig. (2-tailed)	.	5.04E-13	1.76E-10	5.8E-06	3.03E-05	0.002809	0.004382	0.001039	0.004687	0.005051
Sum of Squares and Cross-products	1965.277	984.8065	1029.026	560.1613	426.4129	361.5226	390.9677	370.7935	303.729	284.3032
Covariance	6.360121	3.187076	3.330181	1.81282	1.379977	1.169976	1.265268	1.199979	0.982942	0.920075
N	310	310	310	310	310	310	310	310	310	310

Table 25 - Correlation matrix of Good PR

Chapter 30

<hr>

Stake Holders Satisfaction

The stakeholder concept was developed and championed by R. Edward Freeman in his 'Stake holder theory (1984). Since then this terminology has gained wide acceptance in government, business purpose and practice of strategic management, corporate governance and corporate social responsibility. The word "stakeholder" has become more commonly used these days to mean a person or organization that has a legitimate interest in a project or entity. In discussing the decision-making process for institutions and organizations the concept has been broadened to include everyone with an interest (or "stake") in what the entity does. This includes not only directors or trustees on its governing board, management, employees, customers, vendors, but even members of a community where its offices or factory may affect the local economy or environment. Another definition given by Post, Preston and Sachs (2002) in their theory "Stake holder view', describe stakeholders in a corporation as individuals and constituencies that contribute, either voluntarily or involuntarily, to its wealth- creating capacity and activities, and are thus its potential beneficiaries or risk bearers. This definition is at variance from Freemans as mentioned above.

In the corporate world there is an ongoing debate about whether the firm or company should be managed for stakeholders, stockholders or customers. Proponents in favour of stakeholders base their arguments on the value created by a company by trying to maximize joint outcomes by satisfying the needs of the employees, and wants of the shareholders and customers who are some of the main stakeholders. The combined effects of such a policy are not only additive but even multiplicative. The employees and shareholders both benefit from increased sales which come about by addressing customer wishes in addition to employee, stockholder and other stakeholder's interests. It is not necessary that all stakeholders will also be stockholders e.g CEO who manages the company may not be a stockholder but is very much a stakeholder.

The greatest value of a company is the life space a company creates through its image and brand. By attempting to fulfill the needs and wants of many different stakeholders ranging from the local population and customers to their own employees and owners, companies can enhance their life space by preventing damage to their image and brand. They can prevent losing large amounts of sales and disgruntled customers, as also prevent costly legal expenses. While the stakeholder view has an increased cost, many firms have decided that the concept improves their image, increases sales, and reduces the risks of liability for corporate negligence.

All stakeholders are not equal and different stakeholders are entitled to different considerations depending on the quantum and type of stakes involved in an organization. The groups of stakeholders are thus basic driving forces for any organization. Each group poses special challenges for management, but also provides unique opportunities to obtain competitive advantage. The management must outline a framework/ strategy for organizing the activities of the organization in order to focus clearly on stakeholder satisfaction.

Stake holders can basically be classified as internal and external stakeholders. Internal stakeholders are the employees and the management while others are external stakeholders. The external stakeholders can be local, regional, country specific or global depending upon their geographical location and influence. The management in order to enhance stakeholder satisfaction must take the following actions as given in model below:-

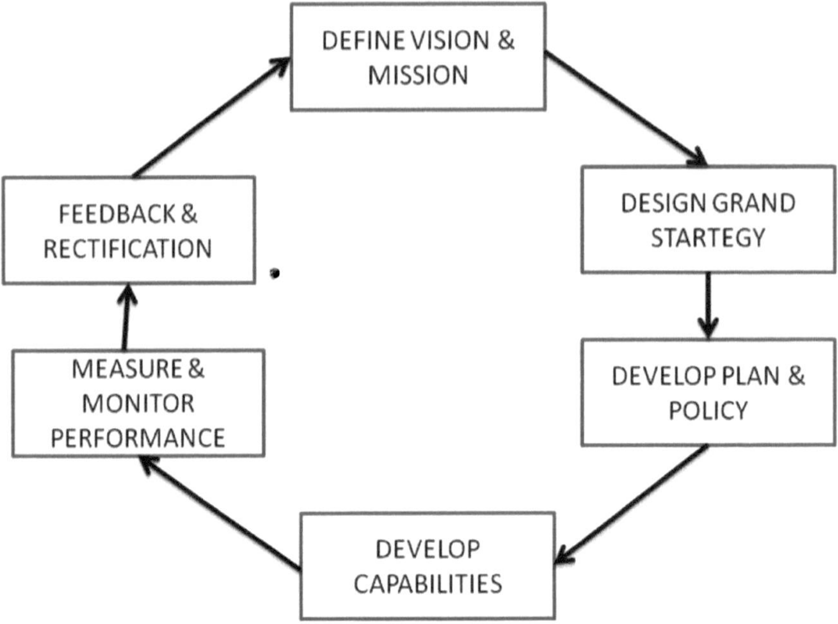

Figure 4 Enhancing stakeholders satisfaction model

(a) Define Vision and Mission. The top management must carry out an environmental scan based on the interests of the stakeholders; forecast the future and give out a vision for the organization. Based on the vision the management must work out the mission statement.

(b) Design a grand strategy. Based on the mission statement the management must carry out SWOT analysis and work out where the company is and where in a given time frame it wants to be. This will give out the strategic gap and the objectives to be achieved. Based on the objectives management must design a strategy to be adopted to fulfill the mission and achieve the set out objectives.

(c) Develop a Plan and Policy. The drivers of change prioritized based on stakeholders requirements obtained earlier are incorporated in designing the plans and policies to meet the desired ends of strategy of the organisation.

(d) Developing Capabilities. The focus of this set of activities is on how the objectives, targets, and programs become translated into literal reality. Management defines the accountability for specific actions within the organisation, and provides the resources to perform these actions. Each person in the organization is required to know their roles and responsibilities in satisfying stakeholder interests.

(e) Measuring and Monitoring Performance. This activity is essential to understand where the organization is and where is it headed in achieving the interests of the stakeholders.

(f) Feedback and Rectification. A good management system carries out reviews at regular intervals to identify strengths, weakness, opportunities and threats based on the feedback from both internal and external stakeholders and then takes corrective measures and completes the cyclic loop of activities.

Relevance to the study

From the study of responses it emerges that stakeholder satisfaction can create for an organization up to 27.65% life space with others in the environment.

Stake holders satisfaction has a reasonably strong and positive correlation with good PR, power projection, ethics, employee satisfaction in that order. The details are as given below:-

	Stake Holders Satisfaction	Good PR	Power Projection	Ethics	Employee Satisfaction
Pearson Correlation	1	0.395088	0.38585	0.285278	0.245402
Sig. (2-tailed)	-	5.04E-13	1.91E-12	3.24E-07	1.24E-05
Sum of Squares and Cross-products	3161.484	984.8065	1429.935	797.0968	665.1935
Covariance	10.23134	3.187076	4.627623	2.579601	2.15273
N	310	310	310	310	310

Table 26 - Relevant correlation of Stake holders satisfaction at organizational level

Satisfied stakeholders become a great source of Good PR and power projection and create a sizeable life space in the environment for the organization.

Chapter 31

Power Projection

Power projection is a term used primarily in American military and political science to refer to the capacity of a state to implement policy by means of force, or the threat thereof, in an area distant from its own territory. The United States Department of Defence, in its publication J1-02: Department of Defense Dictionary of Military and Associated Terms, further defines power projection as the ability of a nation to apply all or some of its elements of national power - political, economic, informational, or military - to rapidly and effectively deploy and sustain forces in and from multiple dispersed locations to respond to crises, to contribute to deterrence, and to enhance regional stability.

Power projection thus emerges as the ability of a nation to apply all or some of its elements of national power to respond to crises and to contribute to deterrence it is extensively used by nation states to create huge life space for themselves. This is more coercive in nature as it involves display of political astuteness, military and technological might. American supremacy today is an outcome of such power projection.

Intrinsically organisations too exert their power by acquiring territories of influence not by their military might but by adopting similar strategies. It is more in the realm of political power that corporate world tries to exert its influence. Political power (imperium in Latin) is a type of power exerted by a group in a society which allows administration of some or all of public resources, including labour, and wealth. Political power can be obtained in several ways. At the nation-state level it can be held by the representatives of national sovereignty through political legitimacy. Political powers can also be wielded by individuals, insurgents, terrorists, or even multinational corporations depending upon the amount of societal influence they have in that nation whether formally or informally. Most corporations are politically savvy and well connected. They are able to influence political decision making. They expand their business by such power.

Relevance to the Study

Power projection does not find favour with the respondents and thus has been ranked very low. Also the respondents feel the amount of life space power projection creates is comparatively less. It is also observed that defence personnel by virtue of their profession give greater relevance to power projection as compared to civilians. The views of civilian and defence personnel on quantum of life space created by power projection are as indicated below:-

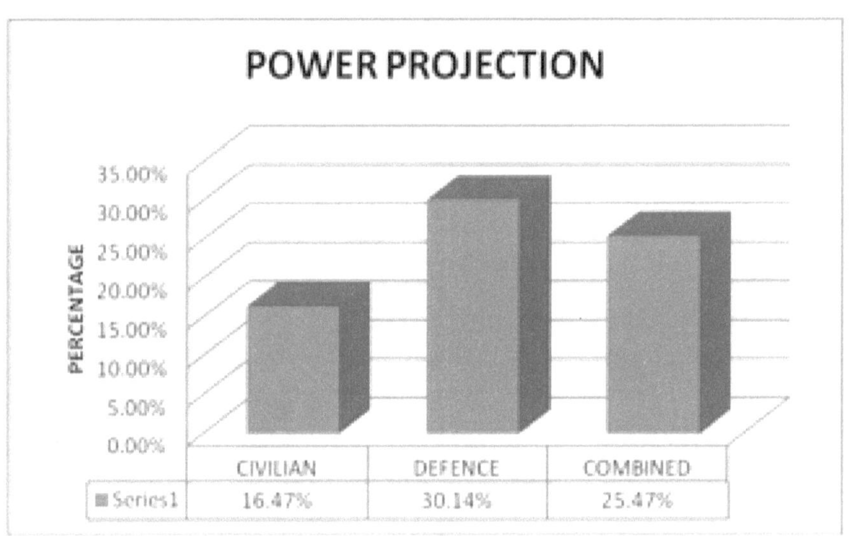

Chart 2 - Life space created by power projection at organizational level

Correlation between power projection and other parameters is as given below:-

	Power Projection	Stake Holders Satisfaction	Good PR	Communication	Ethics	Decision Making
Pearson Correlation	1	0.38585	0.352178	0.296668	0.283147	0.206169
Sig. (2-tailed)	-	1.91E-12	1.76E-10	1.02E-07	3.99E-07	0.000258
Sum of Squares and Cross-products	4344.142	1429.935	1029.026	1068.323	927.3871	557.271
Covariance	14.05871	4.627623	3.330181	3.457355	3.001253	1.803466
N	310	310	310	310	310	310

Table 27 - Relevant correlation of power projection at organizational level

From the Table given above it emerges that power projection has strong and positive correlation with stake holders satisfaction followed by good public relations, communication, ethics and decision making in that order. This summarises that all these factors positively contribute to power projection by nations and organizations.

Power projection also increases with economical and technological might of an organistion.

Chapter 32

Conclusion

Life space management is a daily event, which each individual, group, organizations and nations indulge in order to makes progress. Everyone attempts to create their own space with others so as to extract a favourable situation or position for the self. At individual physical plane of existence life space is an out come of several complex issues like interpersonal relations, sound communications, leadership, motivation, conflict management, power, self concept etc. These issues have been discussed by various behavioural scientists and emerge in the study as the root parameters of life space management applicable to individuals. Similarly effective management team, work culture, effective leadership, employee satisfaction, organizational ethics, decision making, good public relations, stake holders satisfaction and power projection emerge as the parameters that help in creating life space at organizational level. Similarly root parameters of creating life space at national level can be found out. These parameters of creating life space and their management generates insight into behavioural strategies to improve efficiency and productivity, from which certain inferences can be drawn, which support the concept of life space management.

Organisations and nations consist of human beings and every action of the organization/nation is influenced by human nature. It is therefore essential to understand the evolution of human beings and their ultimate purpose of existence. Ancient Indian philosophy mentions evolution of human beings from matter to its highest state of bliss in the panch kosh model of evolution. Human existence based on panch kosh can be classified into three states of existence as shown below:-

PLANES OF EXISTENCE

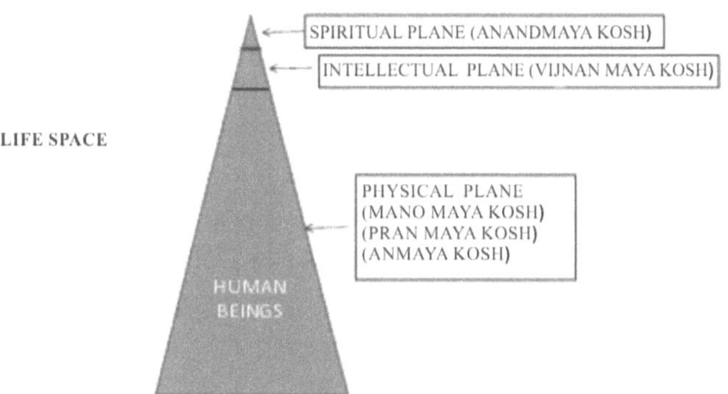

Figure 5 - Planes of human existence

It is observed that vast majority of the population operates at physical plane of existence maybe approximately 98-99%. One to two percent of the population operates at the intellectual plane of existence and one in million operates at the spiritual plane of existence. These figures are a guess estimate and need to be empirically proved. The three planes are prevalent in each individual however their degree of prominence varies from individual to individual. At the physical plane of existence the individual is mired in the web of *maya* (illusion). This influence of *maya* keeps reducing as the human being evolves to higher plane of existence. From the study it emerged that at the physical plane of existence the struggle for creating life space is immense however as the individual rises to higher plane of existence the life space is created on its own. This fact emerges from the fact that Swami Vivekananda creates larger life space than others even though he attained *mahasmadhi* (left physical existence) long back. All spiritual leaders like Jesus, Gautama Buddha, Mahavira, Guru Nanak Dev, Prophet Mohammad, Rama, Krishna, Shankaracharya, Sai Baba of Shirdi, Ram Krishan Paramhans, continue to create life space with their devotees much after they forsake their human bodies. No other human being who operated at physical or intellectual plane has created a life space as much as these great souls have.

Life and Space are still beyond human comprehension. Indian scriptures describe them as an aspect of the divine. In the Upanishads it is mentioned that everything originates and merges back in the Brahman

(Divine Self). Shankaracharya in Brahma Sutra Bhasya describes *prana* (life) as the vital energy and further goes on to describe it as the Brahman. To substantiate it further he mentions that in the Chandogya Upanishad it is mentioned that " All the things proceed towards and merge in Prana and from It they emerge." Since the origin and dissolution of all things is from Prana it proves that Prana and Brahman are one and the same. Similarly in a dialogue between Salvatya and Pravahana Jaivali on goal of the world as given in Chandogya Upnisad, it emerges that Space is the supreme goal. It is the supreme goal as all things originate from space and merge back into space. It is established fact that all things originate from Brahman and merge back into Brahman, therefore Brahman and Space are one and the same. (Swami Gambhirananda, 2000).

As per Sri Aurobindo,(1998) " Inferior man (physical plane) gravitates downwards from mind towards life and body; average mankind (physical plane) dwells constantly in mind limited by and looking towards life and body; superior mankind (intellectual plane) levitates upward either to idealized mentality or pure idea, direct truth of knowledge and spontaneous truth of existence; supreme mankind (spiritual plane) rises to divine beatitude and from that level either goes upward to pure *Sat* and *Parbrahman* or remains to beatify its lower members and raise to divinity in itself and others-this human existence."

As per Indian scriptures struggle for space in an aspect of illusion (*Maya*) especially in the lower planes of existence and hence is transitory in nature. This struggle at lower planes gets compounded due to ego. Greater the ego, greater is the desire for greater physical space. What is not understood is that when an individual de-egoises the self, such a personality becomes permeable and boundless like that of Mahatma Gandhi, Mother Teresa, Ravindranath Tagore, Aurobindo etc. These are examples of how one can raise oneself from the physical plane to the spiritual plane. Also those who exist at physical plane engage themselves in activities to gratify their *indiriyas* or senses. Their behaviour as per Freud is subject to whims of id. These are selfish and transitory in nature and hence limited in space and time. As per Swami Vivekananda all the great system of ethics preach absolute unselfishness as the goal. Any person who attains this goal of unselfishness he no longer remains the little Mr. So and so, he acquires infinite expansion. Unfortunately few achieve this perfection.

Those who are intellectuals they stimulate our minds and create a larger space than the ordinary. But intellect by itself is restrictive in nature. It is a good servant but a bad master. Those who live at physical plane are charmed with *Maya*. *Maya* is ignorance and an intellectual is full of knowledge and as per Swami Vivekananda ignorance is death and knowledge is life. Life is of very little value, if it is a life led in the dark, groping through ignorance and misery. An intellectual converts knowledge into wisdom through internalized contemplation of knowledge. He then can put across a very complex issue in a very simple way. Therefore he attracts our attention and creates a very large space in our hearts and minds.

A person who operates at a spiritual plane creates the maximum space. Sky is the limit for him. Space at spiritual plane is infinite. Take every evolved person e.g. Sri Ram Krishan Paramhans, Prophet, Jesus, Buddha etc. They attained *maha Samadhi* (left physical existence) long back but the space they occupy in our hearts and minds even today is infinite. It is without a beginning and without an end. So for an individual to be effective in life, the individual must embrace spirituality. As per Swami Vivekananda "Spiritual knowledge is the only thing that can destroy our miseries for ever; any other knowledge satisfies wants only for a time."

Can lesser mortals attain spiritual plane. Of course all can with certain effort graduate from the physical to the spiritual plane. When an individual graduates to the spiritual plane a serenity and calmness overcomes his personality and he radiates an aura that draws people far and wide towards him. When he speaks, pearls of wisdom flow out of him, such a person's effectiveness is enhanced million times. So seek self-realization, for a realized soul is the epitome of effectiveness and perfection in life. There are various paths to achieve self-realization like, Karma yoga, Prem yoga, Bhakti yoga and Gyan yoga etc.

An evolved soul becomes a beacon for directing lesser-evolved souls form darkness to light. The space such personality occupies is stabilized and long lasting. The effectiveness of such a soul is immense as it achieves greater perfection while continuing to evolve and grow in the spiritual plane. Therefore each individual must rise above the physical plane of existence and evolve to higher spiritual plane. With rise of individuals to higher planes organizations will also rise and the nation too will rise to higher and higher heights of glory and fame.

BIBLIOGRAPHY

A.C. Bhaktivedanta Swami Prabhupada,Narad-Bhakti –Sutra, The Secrets of The Transdental Love, The Bhakti Vedanta Book Trust, Hare Krishna Land, Juhu, Mumbai, 400049, 2006.

AC Leyton, The Art of Communication, Communication in industry, Pitman Press, UK, 1970.

Bergeret, Jean., Personnalités normales et pathologiques: Les structures mentales, le caractère, les symptômes. Revue française de psychanalyse, 40 (2), 351-370. (1976).

Bert Decker, The Art Of Communicating, Achieving Interpersonal Impact in Business, Viva Books Private Limited, 4262/3 Ansari Road, New Delhi 1100002, 2004.

Bram P. Buunk, Affiliation, Attraction and Close Relationship, Introduction to Social Psychology, A European Perspective, Blackwell Publishers, 108 Cowley Road, Oxford OX4 1JF, UK, 1996

BR Nanda, In Gandhi's footsteps- The Life & Times of Jamuna Lal Bajaj, Oxford University Press, 1990.

Caprara & Cervone, Personality, Determinants, Dynamics, and Potentials, Cambridge University Press,The Edinburg Building, Cambridge, UK, (2000).

Carver,CS, Physical aggression as a function of objective self awareness and attitudes topwards punishment, Journal of eExperimental Social Psychology, 1975

Clark Ronaldh, Einstien, Life & Times, World Publication Company, New York, 1971, (www.princeton.edu.globalcreativitycorp.com)

CR Grindle, Company Efficiency and Human Resources, Who really are the best employees, Hemkunt Press : Publishers, 1-E/15 Patel Road, New Delhi-8, 1969.

Compiled by B.L.Atreya, and translated by Samvid, The Vision and The Way of Vasistha, Published by Samta Books,10 Congress Building, 573, Mount Road,Chennai-600006, 2005.

The Complete Works of Swami Vivekananda, Mayavati Memorial Edition, Vol VIII, Advaita Ashrama, Publication Department, 5 Dehi Entally Road, Kolkata,700014, 2006.

Curt Coffman, Gabriel Gonzalez- Molina,Ph.D. & Ashok Gopal, Follow This Path, Warner Books, Inc, 1271Avenue of The Americas, New York, NY 10020, 2002.

D Amarchand & BJ Jayraj, Corporate Culture and Organisational Effectiveness, Global Business Press, New Delhi, 1992.

Dalton E. MacFarland,Company Efficiency and Human Resources, Who really are the best employees, Hemkunt Press : Publishers, 1-E/15 Patel Road, New Delhi-8, 1969.

David Brooks, Self-control is the key to success, New York Times Service, Tuesday, May 9, 2006

David Finn, Public Relations and Management, Reinhold Publishing Corporation, New York, USA, 1960.

David G Myers, Social Psychology, McGraw – Hill, Inc, New Delhi, 1993

David J Schneider, Social Psychology, Addison- Wesley Publishing Company, Reading Massachuesetts, Menalo Park, California, USA, 1976

David J. Lawless, Effective Management, Social Psychological Approach, Prentice Hall, Inc, Englewood Cliffs, New Jersey, USA, 1972.

Dipankar Gupta. Culture Space and the Nation State. Sage Publications India Pvt Ltd : Greater Kailash, New Delhi, (2000)

Dr Harnam Singh Shan, Sayings Of Guru Nanak, (Originals with english translations), Shiromani Gurudwara Parbandhak Committtee,Amritsar, 2002.

Dr S Ravishankar, Dr RK Mishra, Improving Organisational Effectiveness, Jaico Publishing House, 121, MG Road, Bombay- 400023, 1994.

Edited by Ann Myren & Dorothy Madison, Living At The Sorce, Yoga teacings of Vivekananda, Published by Swami Mumukshananda, Advita Ashram, 5 Dehi Entally Road, Calcutta, 2001.

Edward de bono, The Six Value medals, Vermillion, Random House, UK Ltd, 20 Vauxhall Bridge Road, London SWI V 25 A, 2005.

Elizabeth B. Hurlock, Personality Development,Tata McGraw- hill Publishing Company Ltd, New Delhi, 1976.pp425

Etzioni, Modern Organisations, Prentice Hall, New Delhi, 1965

Extracts from Sri Aurobindo and The Mother, A Practical Guide to Integral Yoga, Sri Aurobindo Ashram Trust, Sri Aurobindo Ashram Press, Pondicherry,1998, pp217& 254

F.G. Fowler & H.W. Fowler, The pocket Oxford Dictionary, of Current English, Oxford University Press, UK, 1961.

Frank Jefkins, Public Relations fpr Your Business, Mercury Books Division of WH Allen & Co. Plc, 44 Hill Street, London W1X8LB, 1987.

Frawney David, Raja Ram, Hidden Horizons – Unearthing 10,000 Years of Indian Culture, April 2006

Fusiler M Subash Durlabji, Cultural Values of Indian managers- An explorationthrough unstructured Interviews, International journal of Value Based management,2001

G. James Francis, Gene Milbourn Jr, Human Behaviour in The Work Environment: Managerial Perspective. Goodyear publishing Company, Inc. santa Monica, California, USA,1980

Gian vittorio Caprarta & Daniel Cervone, Personality, Determinants, Dynamics, and Potentials, Cambridge University Press, , 40 west 20th street, New york, NY 10011-4211, USA, 2000.

Gibson, Ivancevich and Donnelley, Organisations; Structure, Behaviour and Process, Business Publications De Dellon, Texas, (1979)

H. Andrew Michener, John D. DeLamater, Shalom H. Schwartz, Social Psychology, Harcourt Brace Jovanovich, Publishers, Orlando, Florida, USA, 1986.

H. Andrew Michener, John D. DeLamater, Shalom H. Schwartz,Social Psychology, Harcourt Brace Jovanovich, Publishers, Inc, USA, 1986.

Harry Kaufmann, Social Psychology, The Study of Human Interaction, Holt, Rinehart and Winston, Inc, USA, 1973.

Indian Journal of Clinical Psychology,1994

Jayadayal Goyandka, Srimad Bhagwadgita, (With English Translation and Transliteration), Gita Press, Gorakhpur, India, 1991.

Jerry Lopper, The Power of Positive Attitude, The benefits of positive thinking, positive mental attitude and optimism, 03 Feb 2007.

John Bramham, Human Resource Planning, Universities Press (India) Limited, 3-5-819, Hyderguda, Hyderabad, 500 029, 1997.

John M. Wiemann and Howard Giles, Communication in Interpersonal and Social Relationships, Introduction To Social Psychology, A European Perspective,Blackwell Publishers,, 108 Cowley Road, Oxford OX4 1JF, UK, 1997

K Rangaswamy, Self Actualisation and beyond- Union with Universal Self, The highest Motive from Indian Perspective.

Kamala Subramaniam, Mahabharata,Bharatiya Vidya Bhawan, Kulapati Munshi marg, Mumbai, 400007,2004

Kamla Subramanium, Mahabharat, Ch1, After the War, Bhartiya Vidya Bhawan, Kulpati Munshi Marg, Mumbai,-400007, 2004.

Kevin Hoogan, Talk Your Way To the Top, Communication Secrets To Change Your life, Magna Publishing Co. Ltd, Magna House, 100/E, Old Prabha Devi Road, Mumbai, 400025, 2000.

KM Srinivasa, Achieving Excellence in Indian Organisations – New Oppurtunities for psychology and developing society, 1995.

Kurt Lewin , " Field Theory in Social Science," selected theoretical papers, edited by Darwin Cartwright, by Tavistock PublicationsLimited, 11 New Fetter Lne, London, E.C.4, printed in Great Briton by Lowe & Brydone (Printers) Ltd, London, N.W. 10, 1959, pp 28,29, 44 &57

Kurt Lewin, Principles of Topological Psychology, McGraw- Hill book Company, USA, 1936,

Lalchand Doohan' Jigyasu', 1008 Kabir Vani, Nectar of Truth and Knowledge, Manoj Publications, 761, Main Road Burari, Delhi – 110084, 2005

Larry A. Hjelle & Daniel J. Ziegler, Personality Theories, Basic Assumptions, Research, and Applications,Mc Graw Hill, Inc,International edition,New Delhi, 1992.

Lydia Amir, Platos Theory of Love: Rationality as Passion, The Journal of the Society for Philosophy in Practice, Practical Philosophy, Volume 4.3, Nov 2001,pp 6-14

Madhoo Pavaskr & R.R. Kulkarni, Tata Economic Consultancy Services, second India Studies, Communications, Popular Prakashan Private Ltd, 35 C Tardeo Road, Popular Press Bldg, Bomby, 400034, 1978.

Manibhai, (An Out line of Integral Yoga), A Practical Guide To Integral Yoga, Extracts compiled from the writings of Sri Aurobindo and the Mother, Sri Aurobindo Ashram, Pondicherry,1998

Miles Hewstone, Wolfgang Strobe, Geoffrey M. Stephenson, Introduction to Social Psychology, A European Perspective, Blackwell Publishers, Inc, 108 Cowley Road, Oxford OX4 1JF, UK, 1997

MN Mishra & BL Mathur, Organisational Effectiveness, RBSA Publishers, S.M.S. Highway Jaipur-302003, 1997.

Mohini M. Chatterji,F.T.S., Viveka-Cudamani, or Crest –Jewel of Wisdom of Sri Samkaracarya, The Theosophical Publishing House, Adyar, Chennai,1999.

Nicolas Nova, CRAFT Research Report_1, "Socio-cognitive functions of space in collaborative settings : a literature review about Space, Cognition and Collaboration

Norman Vincent Peale,The Power of Positive Thinking for young People, Vermillion, Random House UK Ltd, 20, Vauxhall Bridge Road, London SW1V2SA, UK, 1997,

Norman Vincent Peale,The Power of Positive Thinking, Vermillion, Random House UK Ltd, 20, Vauxhall Bridge Road, London SW1V2SA, UK, 1998,

Paddy O' Brien, Positive Management Assertiveness for Managers, Reaserch Press, Post Box 7208, 212 Vardaan House, 7/28 Ansari Road, New Delhi, 110002, 1992.

Paul E. Mott, The Characteristics of Effective Organizations, Harper &

Row, Publishers, USA, 1972.

Paul Hersey, Kenneth H Blanchard, Dewey E Johnson, Management of Organisational Behaviour, Leading human resources, Prentice – Hall of India,New Delhi 110001, 2002.

Petty.R.E. and J.T. Cacioppo, Attitudes and persuasion; Classic and contemporary approaches, Dubuque,IA: William C. Brown, 1981

Philip G Zimbardo, Ebbe B. ebbesen, Christina Masalch, Influencing Attitudes and Changing Behaviour, Addison – Wesley Publishing Company Inc, USA, 1997

Pierre Rousselot, The Problem of Love in the Middle Ages: A Historical Contribution. Trans. Alan Vincelette (Milwaukee: Marquette Univ. Press, 2001).

Prof Sk Chakraborty, Values and Ethics for Organizations, Theory and Practice, Oxford University Press, YMCA Library Building, Jai Singh Road, New Delhi-110001,1999,pp07.

Published by Swami Mumukshananda, Selections from The Complete Works of Swami Vivekananda,Advaita Ashram, Publication department, 5 Dehi Entally Road, Calcutta 700014, 1998.

Richard M. Steers, Organisational Effectiveness A Behavioural View, Goodyear Publishing Company, Inc. Santa Monica, California, 1977.

Robert A Baron & Donn Byrne, Social Psychology, Eighth Edition, Princeton – Hall of India Private Limited, M-97, Cannaught Circus, New Delhi-110001, Jan 1998

Roger D' aprix, Communication for Change, Connecting the Workplace with the marketplace. Jossey – Bass, 989 market Street, san Francisco, CA 94103-1741, USA, 1996.

Rokeach M. Beliefs, Attitudes and Values, Jossey Bass, SanFrancisco, USA, 1968.

Scot M. Cutlip & Allen H. Center, Effective Public Relations, Prentice-Hall, International, Englewood Cliffs, New Jersey, 07632, 1982.

Seligman, Martin E. P., Authentic Happiness , Positive Psychology Values in Action (VIA) Classification of Strengths and Virtues,New York: Free Press,2002. September 2003, pdf document, accessed on 23 sep 05, pp20

SK Chakraborty& Pradip Bhattacharya, Human Values, The Tagorean Panaroma, (Translations from Shantiniketan), New Age International (P) Limited,Publishers,4835/24 Ansari Road, New Delhi, 110002, 1999.

SK Chakraborty, Managerial Transformation by Values, A corporate Pilgrimage, Sage Publications India Pvt Ltd, M-32,Greater Kailash Market, Part 1, New Delhi, 110048, !993.

SK Chakraborty, Values and Ethics for Organisations, Theory and Prqactice,Oxford University Presss, YMCA Building,Jai Singh Road, New Delhi 110001, 1999.

Sri Aurobindo, A Practical Guide To Integral Yoga, (Extracts Compiled from the writings of Sri Aurobindo and The Mother), Sri Aurobindo Ashram Press, Pondicherry,1998.

Sri Aurobindo, The Life Divine, Sri Aurobindo Ashram Publication Department, Sri Aurobindo Ashram Press, Pondicherry, 1997,181pp pp,199

Subhash Sharma, Indian Ethos, Indian Culture,and Indian Management,- TowardsNew Frontiers in Management Thinking, 2005

Swami Chetananada, Swami Vivekananda, Vedanta Voice of Freedom, Advaita Aharama Publication Department, Dehi Entally Road, Kolkatta – 700014,2007,pp43.

Swami Gambhirananda, "Brahma Sutra Bhasya of Shankaracharya," translated, Advaita Ashrama,Publication department. 5 Delhi Entally Road, Calcutta, 700014, Seventh Impression, January 2000, pp82 &83.

Swami Jagadatmananda, Translated by Thirumaleshwar Bhat, Learn To Live Volume 1, Sri Ramkrishna Math Mylapore, Chennai, 2004, pp122

Swami Nityaswarupananda, Astvakra samhita, Advaita Ashrama, publication department, 5 Dehi Entally Road, Kolkatta 700014, twelfth impression , January 2004, pp100.

Swami Ranganathananda, "The Message of the Upanishads, "Isa Upanishad", Bhartiya Vidya Bhavan, Kulpati Munshi marg,Bombay,400007, Seventh edition,1993.pp 63, 101/102

Swami Sunirmalananda, Insights into Vedanta, Tattvabodha, Sri Ramakrishna math Chennai, India, 2005,pp10.

Swami Vivekananda, Jnana Yoga, The Yoga of Knowledge, Advaita Ashrama, Publication department. 5 Delhi Entally Road, Calcutta, 700014, Twentieth Impression, May 1997,pp 115-117

Swami Vivekananda, Selections From The Comlete Works of Swami Vivekananda, Published by Swami Mumukshananda, Advaita Ashrama, (Publication Department), 5 Dehi Entally Road, Calcutta, 700014, 1998.

Swami Yuktanand, Value Vision, Vivekananda Nidhi, The Institute of Value Orientation & Environmental Education, 149/1E Rasbehari Avenue, Kolkata, 700029,2003.

T.M. Lillico, Managerial Communication, Pergmon Press Ltd, Headington Hill Hall, Oxford<UK, 1972.

The Eternal Wisdom, Central sayings of Great Sages of all Times, Sri Aurobindo Ashram, Pondicherry, 1995.

The Intersubjective Geometry of Social Space. Contributors: Bibb Latané - author. Journal Title: Journal of Communication. Volume: 46. Issue: 4. Publication Year: 1996. Page Number22, accessed on 23 April 2004).

Uday Shanker, Personality Development, Atma Ram & Sons, (H.O.) Kashmere Gate, Delhi- 110006, 1980.

V.S.P-.Rao and P.S. Narayana, Organisation Theory and Behaviour, Konark Publishers, Pvt Ltd, A-149, Main Vikas Marg, New Delhi, 110092, 2000.

Walter Mischel, Introduction to Personality, Holt, Rinehart an

Internet Sites Accessed

http://www.KURTLEWIN\individual performance enhancement.htm accessed on 05 Aug 2003.

http://www.jestmanagement.co.uk/content/individual_effectiveness accessed on 18/05/08

R.J. Rummel , Understanding Conflict and War: vol. 1: The Dynamic Psychological Field, Chapter 3, Psychological Field Theories, http://www.hawaii.edu/powerkills/DPF.CHAP3.HTM   accessed on 19/05/08

Wikepedia University site http://en.wikipedia.org/wiki/Lebensraum accessed on 19 May 05.

http://history1900s.about.com/library/holocaust/aa110899.htm   accessed on 19 May 05.

Ian Williams, The Beginning of time, University of Hertfordshire, Astronomy, Astronomy Unbound Page© Stuart Clark 1993, http://www.herts.ac.uk/astro ub/a/4 ub.html accessed on 23 Jan 05.

Millie V Jones , Class Bios of Kurt Lewin,

http://www.utexas.edu/coc/journalism/SOURCE/j363/lewin.html, accessed on 18 May 05.Chapter V, Causal Interconnections in Psychology the Historical and the Systematic Concept of Causality,

http://www.questia.com/PM.qst;jsessionid=BNkNgY32RBqd yJTGrCLnFR1LJdTQFWpmQTdTHFLJK1lbyG59yNcX!-2081808426?a=o&d=1043431 accessed on 05 Jun o5.

http://www.infed.thinkers/et.lewin.htm   accessed on 23 May 05

Chapter III of PRINCIPLES OF TOPOLOGICAL PSYCHOLOGY, BY KURT LEWIN Professor of Child Psychology, Iowa Child Welfare Research Station, University of Iowa ,TRANSLATED BY FRITZ HEIDER Assistant Professor, Department of Education, Smith College AND GRACE M. HEIDER FIRST EDITION FOURTH IMPRESSION

http://www.questia.com/PM.qst;jsessionid=BNkNgY32RBqd yJTGrCLnFR1LJdTQFWpmQTdTHFLJK1lbyG59yNcX!-2081808426?a=o&d=1043431   accessed on 23 Nov 04Chapter IV, Content and extent of the Psychological Life Space,

http://www.questia.com/PM.qst;jsessionid=BNkNgY32RBqd yJTGrCLnFR1LJdTQFWpmQTdTHFLJK1lbyG59yNcX!-2081808426?a=o&d=1043431 accessed on 05 Jun o5.

Victor Daniels Website in The Psychology Department at Sonoma state University,Kurt Lewin Notes, http://www.sonoma.edu/users/d/daniels/lewinnotes.html accessed on 25 May 05.

Wikipedia, the free encyclopedia, Origin of life,http://en.wikipedia.org/wiki/Life accessed on 19 June 05

The American Heritage® Stedman's Medical Dictionary, Houghton Mifflin Company2002

http://dictionary.reference.com/search?q=life, accessed 23 August 2004

Claus Emmeche, Defining Life, Explaining Emergence, Center for the Philosophy of Nature and Science Studies,Niels Bohr Institute,Blegdamsvej 17,DK-2100 Copenhagen Denmark,

http://www.nbi.dk/~emmeche/cePubl/97e.defLife.v3f.html, accessed 29 Mar 2004

http:// www.lifeuniverse.com/noflash/Lifedefinition-04-01.html accessed on 23 March 2003 Seth Shostak, " The Meaning Of Life," Astronomer, Project Phoenix, posted on 29 Aug 2002 at http://www.space.com

Definitions,http://www.meaningoflife.i12.com/conclusion.htm, accessed 25 May 2005.

Avshalom C. Elitzur, "C'EST LA VIE: A PHYSICIST'S DEFINITION," Unit for Interdisciplinary Studies, Bar-Ilan University, 52900 Ramat-Gan , Israel , http://faculty.biu.ac.il/~elitzua/life-def.htm accessed on 28/01/05

Definition of life(Brainy dictionary) http://www.brainydictionary.com/words/li/life184840.html accessed on 19 June 05.

Life's Working Definition: Does It Work?,By The Staff of Astrobiology Magazine http://www.space.com/scienceastronomy/astrobiolife_030415 . html, posted: 07:30 am ET, 15 April 200

http://www.space.com/scienceastronomy/astrobio_life_030415.html. accessed on 29 Mar 2004

Joseph Morales, The Definition of Life, Psychozoan: A Journal of Culture, 1998 http:// www.lifeuniverse.com/noflash/Lifedefinition-04-01.html, accessed on 29 Mar 2005.

Mark A. Bedau, Abstract in "Four Puzzles about Life,"Reed College, 3203 SE Woodstock Blvd., Portland OR 97202, USA, Email: ab@reed.edu,,

http://www.reed.edu/~mab/papers/4.puzzles.htm accessed on 23 October 2004

http://www.thefreedictionary.com/space accessed on 30 Dec2004

Architectural Intervention Collaboration,Project 01: Architecture and Space, http://a.parsons.edu/~tarazi/ArchInter_Pr01_2.html accessed on 09 Nov 05.

David Kirsh, " A Few Thoughts on Cognitive Overload", Dept. of Cognitive Science, Univ. California, San Diego,La Jolla, CA 92093-0515,kirsh@ucsd.edu,

http://icl-server.ucsd.edu/~kirsh/Articles/Overload/published.html accessed on 04 N0v 05.

Maier, H. W , INTERNATIONAL CHILD AND YOUTH CARE NETWORK, "Today," Thinking about the Life Space,14 DECEMBER 2000, http://www.cyc-net.org/today2000/today001214.html down loaded on 23 accessed 08 Jul04.

Nicolas Nova, CRAFT Research Report_1, "Socio-cognitive functions of space in collaborative settings : a literature review about Space, Cognition and Collaboration, September 2003, pdf document, downloaded on 23 sep 05. , pp20,pp,25

Pinhas Ben - Zvi Kant on space an article in Philosophy Now a magazine 2005 .http://www.philosophynow.org/issue49/49benzvi.htm accessed on 07 NOV 05.Chapter viii,The psychological worlds and the physical world, lifes working definition: does it work? by the staff of astrobiology magzine,

http://www.   Space.com/scienceastronomy/astrbio_life   030415.html. posted 07.30 am ET, 15 April 2003.

http://www.philosophynow.org/issue49/49benzvi.htm accessed on 07 NOV 05 Mildred L G Shaw & Brian R Gaines, Kelly's " Geometry of Psychological Space" and its significance for Cognitive Modelling, Knowledge Science Institute, University of Calgary,Calgary, Alberta, Canada T2N 1N4,{mildred, gaines}@cpsc.ucalgary.ca,(from The New Psychologist, 23-31, October, 1992) ,

http://ksi.cpsc.ucalgary.ca/articles/NewPsych92/ accessed on 26 Oct 2005Cognitive space, From Wikipedia, the free encyclopedia,

http://en.wikipedia.org/wiki/Cognitive_space accessed ON 03 Nov 05.

http://www.philosophynow.org/issue49/49benzvi.htm accessed on 07 NOV 05.More about the narrative approach,

http://www.marathon.uwc.edu/psychology/307_more_narrative.htm accessed on 23 March 2005. "Social space",From Wikipedia, the free encyclopedia.

http://en.wikipedia.org/wiki/Social_space accessed on 29 Oct 05. The Intersubjective Geometry of Social Space. Contributors: Bibb Latané - author. Journal Title: Journal of Communication. Volume: 46. Issue: 4. Publication Year: 1996. Page Number: 26. accessed on 23 April 2004

http://www.questia.com/PM.qst?a=o&d=96517607 accessed 10 Apr 04 R.J. Rummel, "Understanding conflict and war: vol. 1: the dynamic psychological field," chapter 24, The Sociocultural Spaces*, 24.2 THE CULTURAL SPACE,

http://www.mega.nu:8080/ampp/rummel/dpf.chap24.htm accessed on 30 Oct 05. Robert M Young, "Mental Space," Chapter Two, 'CULTURAL SPACE,'

http://human-nature.com/mental/chap2.html accessed on 30 OCT 05

http://en.wikipedia.org/wiki/Space accessed on 02 Feb 07 Nicolas Nova, CRAFT Research Report_1, "Socio-cognitive functions of space in collaborative settings : a literature review about Space, Cognition and Collaboration, September 2003, pdf document, downloaded on 23 sep 05.pp06.

Narrative   Space: Descriptions,   http://www.narrativespace.com/ descriptions.html accessed on 21 March 2006.

http://en.wikipedia.org/wiki/Philosophy_of_space_and_time accessed on 02 feb 07

http://encyclopedia.laborlawtalk.com/Space accessed 22/09/05 Robert M. Young, Chapter Three, "MENTAL SPACE," Online Archive, Center For Psychotherapeutic Studies, Published in Artificial Life 4 (1998): 125-140.

http://www.shef.ac.uk/~psysc/mental/chap3.html , accessed on 21 Oct 04. Robert M Young, Mental Space, Preface, Process Press Ltd,26 Freegrove Road,London N7 9RQ, 1994, http://www.human-nature.com/mental/ preface.html accessed on 04 Feb 07.

Adobe acrobat, pdf, 'Mental %20 spaces(1)' , Mental Spaces by Gilles Fauconnier, This article summarizes and reproduces parts of Fauconnier (1985,1997), Fauconnier & Turner (2002) and a range of articles by severalresearchers, presented on the web at mentalspace,net. cogsci. ucsd.edu/~faucon/151/mental spaces.pdf accessed ON 06 FEB 07 http://www.seedwiki.com/wiki/parametric_design/mental_space_statment?wpid=207536 accessed on 06 Feb 07.

http://en.wikipedia.org/wiki/Spacetime accessed on 11 Feb 07. Hans Reichenbach (1891-1953), The Internet Encyclopaedia of Philosophy,

http://www.iep.utm.edu/r/reichenb.htm accessed on 16 Feb 07.

http://a.parsons.edu/~tarazi/ArchInter_Pr01_2.html accessed on 09 Nov 05.

Maier, H. W , INTERNATIONAL CHILD AND YOUTH CARE NETWORK, "Today," Thinking about the Life Space,14 DECEMBER 2000, http://www.cyc-net.org/today2000/today001214.html. accessed on 23 Jul 04.

http://www.psychology.sbc.edu/Kurt%20Lewin.htm accessed on 25Feb 07

http://www.questia.com/PM.qst?a=o&d=1043431   Chapter III, pp14, accessed on 25 Feb 07 R.J. Rummel, " UNDERSTANDING CONFLICT AND WAR: VOL. 1:THE DYNAMIC PSYCHOLOGICAL FIELD", Chapter 26,Intentions And The Intentional Field* http://www.mega.nu:8080/ampp/rummel/dpf.chap26.htm accessed on 30 Oct05

Timothy E. Jordan, "Field force dynamics, policy adoption, and educational change in secondary classrooms of the Rio Grande Valley," (doctorate in Educational Leadership), Graduate School of the University of Texas - Pan American. CHAPTER VIII,THE PSYCHOLOGICAL WORLDS AND THE PHYSICAL WORLD, Life's Working Definition: Does It Work?,By The Staff of Astrobiology Magazine

http://www.space.com/scienceastronomy/astrobio_life_030415.html, posted: 07:30 am ET, 15 April 2003 Chapter VIII, Life's Working Definition: Does It Work?,By The Staff of Astrobiology Magazine

http://www.space.com/scienceastronomy/astrobio_life_030415.html, posted: 07:30 am ET, 15 April 2003 Chapter VI, Life's Working Definition: Does It Work?,By The Staff of Astrobiology Magazine http://www.space.com/scienceastronomy/astrobio_life_030415.html, posted: 07:30 am ET, 15 April 2003 Chapter XII, Life's Working Definition: Does It Work?,By The Staff of Astrobiology Magazine

http://www.space.com/scienceastronomy/astrobio_life_030415.html, posted: 07:30 am ET, 15 April 2003 Chapter X, Life's Working Definition:

Does It Work?,By The Staff of Astrobiology Magazine

http://www.space.com/scienceastronomy/astrobio_life_030415.html, posted: 07:30 am ET, 15 April 2003 Chapter XV, Life's Working Definition: Does It Work?,By The Staff of Astrobiology Magazine http://www.space.com/scienceastronomy/astrobio_life_030415.html, posted: 07:30 am ET, 15 April 2003

http://www.brainyquote.com/words/ch/character142889.html   accessed on 13/04/08

http://www.merriam-webster.com/dictionary/character   accessed   on 13/04/08

http://216.93.167.235/dictionary/meaning/character/   accessed   on 13/04/08

http://encarta.msn.com/dictionary_1861695812/character.html   accessed on 13/04/08

http://www.newadvent.org/cathen/03584b.htm accessed on 13/04/08

http://www.answers.com/topic/character   accessed on 13/04/08 Father Knuckles, Personality vs Character,

http://johnnyknuckles.blogspot.com/2004/06/personality-vs-character. html Thursday, June 03, 2004, accessed on 13/04/08

http://www.collegevalues.org/articles.cfm?a=1&id=1141   accessed   on 13/04/08\

http://www.answers.com/topic/personality?cat=health   accessed   on 18/04/08

http://www.answers.com/library/Sports Science and Medicine - cid-60986 accessed on 18/04/08

http://wilderdom.com/personality/L5-1WhatIsPersonality.html accessed on 18/04/08

http://www.telegraph.co.uk/earth/main.jhtml?xml=/earth/2007/09/11/ sciface111.xml accessed on 18/04/08

http://www.psitek.net/pages/PsiTekTSOS9.html   accessed on 18/04/08 Bruce M. Meglino and Elizabeth C. Ravlin, Individual Values in Organizations: Concepts, Controversies, and Research, University of

South Carolina

http://jom.sagepub.com/cgi/content/abstract/24/3/351   accessed on 22/04/08

http://www.collegevalues.org/articles.cfm?a=1&id=1141   accessed on 13/04/08

www.positivepsychology.org   accessed on13/04/08 Remez Sasson ,The Power of Positive Thinking,

http://www.successconsciousness.com/index_000009.htm   accessed on 05 Mar 08. Roy Posner,The Power of Personal Attitudes

http://www.gurusoftware.com/GuruNet/Personal/Topics/Attitudes.htm accessed on 06/03/08

http://www.selfgrowth.com/articles/Hansen1.html accessed on 06/03/08

http://lucymacdonald.typepad.com/positive_perspective_quot/   accessed on 05Mar08.

http://dictionary.die.net/attitude accessed on 31/03/08

http://en.wikipedia.org/wiki/Attitude_(psychology) accessed on 31/03/08

http://www.psych.umn.edu/courses/spring06/borgidae/psy5202/images/ attitude%20definitions.pdf accessed on 31/03/08

http://www.wow4u.com/attitude/   accessed on 05Mar 08

http://positiveattitude.in/   accessed on 06Mar08

http://www.charminghealth.com/applicability/negative-attitude.htm accessed on 06 Mar08

http://www.successconsciousness.com/index_000009.htm   accessed on 05 Mar 08.

http://www.personal-development.com/chuck/negativethinking.htm accessed on 05/04/08 Rick Nauert, and John M. Grohol, A Negative Attitude is Contagious

http://psychcentral.com/news/2007/10/05/a-negative-attitude-is-contagious/1374.html ,October 9, 2007, (accessed on 05/04/08)

http://www.charminghealth.com/applicability/negative-attitude.htm

accessed on 05/04/08 Thomas Young, MBA, Everything Starts with Attitude,719-481-4040, tom@intuitivewebsites.com ,326 All Sky Drive,Colorado Springs, CO 80921

http://www.salestrainingplus.com/salesmark/articles/attitude.htm. accessed on 05 Apr 2008

http://www.livinglifefully.com/negattitude.htm accessed on 05/04/08

http://www.positiveattitudemtg.com/ accessed on 03/04/08

http://www.healthandyoga.com/html/news/yoga_positive.html accessed on 03Apr 08

http://www.successconsciousness.com/positive_attitude.htm accessed on 05Mar 08 Remez Sasson, Positive Thinking Your Key to Success,

http://www.successconsciousness.com/index_00003a.htm accessed on 05Mar 08

http://www.answers.com/topic/communication?cat=technology accessed on 17/04/08 Jean Claude Burgelman, Traveling with Communication Technologies in Space, Time, and Everyday Life: An Exploration of Their Impact, First Monday, volume 5, number 3, (March 2000),

URL: http://firstmonday.org/issues/issue5_3/burgelman/index.html

http://findarticles.com/p/articles/mi_m0843/is_n5_v16/ai_9009902 accessed on 18/04/08

http://factiva.com/infopro/resources/Unit10EffectCommResources.doc accessed on 18/04/08

http://www.answers.com/topic/tact accessed on 05/05/08 The American Heritage® Dictionary of the English Language, Fourth Edition copyright ©2000 by Houghton Mifflin Company. Published by Houghton Mifflin Company. Updated in 2003.

http://www.thefreedictionary.com/tact accessed on 05/05/08

http://www.merriam-webster.com/dictionary/tact accessed on 05/05/08

http://www.yourdictionary.com/tact accessed on 05/05/08

http://dictionary.die.net/tact accessed on 05/05/08 The Essentials of Communicating with Tact and Finesse,Detailed Overview/

Outline,http://www.seminarinformation.com/qqbpbn/the-essentials-of-communicating-with-tact-and-finesse   accessed on 05/05/08 Holly Bennett, Learning to Be Tactful, The ability to be tactful is a big developmental step,

http://www.todaysparent.com/schoolage/behaviordevelopment/article.jsp?content=1064244&page=1 accessed on 05/05/08 Self-management, From Wikipedia, the free encyclopedia

http://en.wikipedia.org/wiki/Self-management accessed on 30/04/08

http://www.answers.com/topic/self-control accessed on 30/04/08

http://www.foundationsforfreedom.net/Topics/Parenting/Parenting04_Self-Control.html accessed on 30/04/08

http://www.sfgate.com/cgibin/article.cgi?f=/c/a/2006/05/09/EDGFGINST41.DTL&hw=david+brooks&sn=002&sc=613   accessed on 25/04/08 Developing Self-Control in our Children Self control, Wikipedia, the free encyclopedia

http://en.wikipedia.org/wiki/Self_control   accessed on 25/04/08 Self-control strategies

http://www.minddisorders.com/Py-Z/Self-control-strategies.html accessed on 30/04/08 Self Management Strategies,

http://www.nexus.edu.au/Divisions/curriculum/clp/VacationLiteracy/smintro.htm   accessed on 30/04/08 Mark Dombeck, Ph.D. and Jolyn Wells-Moran, Ph.D. ,Time Management and Organization, Updated: Jun 29th 2006,

http://www.mentalhelp.net/poc/view_doc.php?type=doc&id=9770&cn=353 accessed on 30/04/08 Edward J. O'Keefe, Ph.D. & Donna S. Berger, M.A. SELF-MANAGEMENT FOR COLLEGE STUDENTS: The ABC Approach

http://parthill.com/ accessed on 30/04/08 Scott Langley, Prof. Montgomery, Manipulating People -- Where to Draw the Line7/30/92

http://www.scottlangley.com/writing/ethics.htm accessed on 25/04/08b

http://www.answers.com/topic/manipulation?cat=biz-fin   accessed on 25/04/08 http://onlinedictionary.datasegment.com/word/manipulation   accessed on 25/04/08

http://dictionary.die.net/manipulation   accessed on 25/04/08 Martin Avis, Kickstart Today, Manipulating people:New Information,

http://www.kickstartdaily.com/blog/index.php?/archives/239-Manipulating-people.html   accessed on   25/04/08   Controlling Personalities in the Church: Manipulation Techniques and Your Defenses

http://dory.typepad.com/wittenberg_gate/2005/07/controlling_per.html accessed on 25/04/08

http://gobaarticles.blogspot.com/2007/05/personality-and-charisma.html accessed on 21/04/08

http://en.wikipedia.org/wiki/Charisma   accessed on 24/04/08

http://en.wikipedia.org/wiki/Charismatic_authority accessed on 24/04/08 Thomas Robbins,Charisma,Encyclopedia of Religion and Society, Hartford Institute for Religion Research, Hartford Seminary, (William H. Swatos, Jr. Editor),

http://hirr.hartsem.edu/ency/charisma.htm accessed on 24/04/08ARISMA

http://news.bbc.co.uk/1/hi/magazine/4579681.stm accessed on 24/04/08 Gordon Marshall, Charisma, A Dictionary of Sociology, Oxford University Press, 1998.

http://www.encyclopedia.com/doc/1O88-charisma.html   accessed on 21/04/08 Len Oakes, Prophetic Charisma: The Psychology of Revolutionary Religious Personalities, Book Review, Sociology of Religion, Winter, 1998 by Jane Marie Pinzino, Syracuse University Press, NY, USA, 1997,

http://findarticles.com/p/articles/mi_m0SOR/is_/ai_53590319   accessed on 21/04/08

http://www.leadershipthatworks.com/Articles/Charisma.htm accessed on 21/04/08

http://www.answers.com/topic/charisma?cat=technology   accessed on 21/04/08 Wayne Parker, http://workstar.net/library/charisma.htm accessed on 24/04/08 http://en.wikipedia.org/wiki/Charisma accessed on 24/04/08

http://encarta.msn.com/dictionary_/charisma.html accessed on 21/04/08

http://www.merriam-webster.com/dictionary/charisma   accessed   on 21/04/08

http://www.yourdictionary.com/charisma   accessed on 21/04/08 Carlin Flora, The X-Factors of Success, Article ID: 3751,Psychology Today Magazine, May/Jun 2005, Last Reviewed 23 Oct 2007

http://www.psychologytoday.com/articles/pto-20050502-000001.html accessed on 24/04/08

http://news.bbc.co.uk/1/hi/magazine/4579681.stm accessed on 21/04/08 Jake, Science, Personality Development, 2005,

http://recently.rainweb.net/hive/851/ accessed on 24/04/08

http://www.answers.com/topic/charisma?cat=technology   accessed on 21/04/08 Joe Love, How To Become a Charismatic Leader,2005.

http://ezinearticles.com/?How-To-Become-a-Charismatic-Leader&id=99862   accessed on 21/04/08 Gifts of Revelation,Section8,

http://www.xtremexa.org/resources/Notes/bodyministry8.htm   accessed on 21/04/08 Dharmacari Naagapriya, Pre-Doctrinal Buddhism in the Sutta-Nipaata: A Psychological Portrait of the early Buddhist Saint.

http://www.westernbuddhistreview.com/vol4/early_buddhist_saint.html accessed on 21/04/08 Love, From Wikipedia, the free encyclopedia

http://en.wikipedia.org/wiki/Love accessed on 26/04/08

http://www.explorelove.co.uk/love_definition.htm accessed on 26/04/08

http://www.merriam-webster.com/dictionary/love accessed on 26/04/08

http://www.yourdictionary.com/love accessed on 26/04/08 Definition of true love,

http://www.explorelove.co.uk/love_definition.htm accessed on 26/04/08 Dawson McAllister Live , What is true love and how do you know when you have found it?, Copyright © 1997,

http://christiananswers.net/q-dml/dml-y030.html   accessed on 26/04/08

Some Other Writers on Love, Chapter 36

http://www.akat.com/MeaningOfLove/chapter36.html   accessed on
08/05/08 David, Concise Definition Of True Love,October 9, 2007,
http://faceofgod.wordpress.com/2007/10/09/a-concise-definition-of-
true-love/ accessed on 26/04/08 Rachna Gupta, Definition of Love:
What is Love, Published: 0/18/2007,

http://www.buzzle.com/articles/definition-of-love-what-is-love.html
accessed on 26/04/08 True love,

http://peoplerelationships.syl.com/loverelationships/truelove   accessed
on 26/04/08 Jason Kreag Graduate Student, Center on Philanthropy at
Indiana University, Altruism

http://www.learningtogive.org/papers/index.asp?bpid=3   accessed on
11/05/08 Altruism,

http://www.answers.com/topic/altruism accessed on 11/05/08

http://www.thefreedictionary.com/altruism   accessed on 11/05/08

http://www.merriam-webster.com/dictionary/altruism   accessed on
11/05/08

http://encarta.msn.com/dictionary_1861584974/altruism.html   accessed
on 11/05/08 Altruism, Wikipedia, the free encyclopedia, http://
en.wikipedia.org/wiki/Altruism   accessed on 11/05/08 Ven. Thubten
Chodron, Advantages of Bodhicitta – Part 3 and Developing Equanimity
– Preliminary to Cultivating Bodhicitta (lightly edited transcript), © at
Dharma Friendship Foundation, Seattle. 21 Apr 93

http://www.thubtenchodron.org/GradualPathToEnlightenment/outline.
html accessed on 11/05/08 Respect, Wikipedia, the free encyclopedia,

http://en.wikipedia.org/wiki/Respect   accessed on 14/05/08 Houghton
Mifflin Company, The American Heritage Dictionary of the English
Language, Fourth Edition, Published by Houghton Miffin Company,
Updated in 2003.

http://www.thefreedictionary.com/respecthttp://www.thefreedictionary.
com/respect accessed on 14/05/08 Collins Essential English Dictionary
2nd Edition 2006 © HarperCollins Publishers 2004, 2006 http://www.

thefreedictionary.com/respecthttp://www.thefreedictionary.com/respect   accessed on 14/05/08

http://www.merriam-webster.com/dictionary/respect   accessed on 14/05/08 From Wikipedia, the free encyclopediaFor http://en.wikipedia.org/wiki/Respect accessed on 14/05/08 eHow Business Editor, How to Gain Respect as a Leader,

http://www.ehow.com/how_2099435_gain-respect-as-leader.html accessed on 14/05/08 Tejvan Pettinger, How to Gain the Respect of Others, February 20th, 2008,

http://www.srichinmoybio.co.uk/blog/life/how-to-gain-the-respect-of-others/   accessed on 14/05/08 What Is the Definition of Respect? 08 Dec 2006 http://www.blurtit.com/q205444.html   accessed on 14/05/08 Bibliography Ch V Open systems and organisation theories Chapter 11. A unified open systems model for explaining organisational change

http://epress.anu.edu.au/info_systems/mobile_devices/ch11s03.html accessed on 11 jul 08 Jim R. Macnamara BA, MA, FPRIA, AFAMI, CPM,The Impact of PR on the Media

http://www.carma.com/research/Impact(A4).pdf accessed on 21 May 08. ORGANISATIONAL COMMUNICATION,

http://www.manage.gov.in/eei/teaching/organ.htm   accessed on 24 May 08. Organisational Communication , The Role of HR,

http://www.flipkart.com/organisational-communication-role-hr-professional/8179923835-5v23fakz6f   accessed on 24 May 08. SR Nair, http://www.kma.org.in/man_two.htm   accessed on 24 May 08.

http://www.answers.com/topic/communication?cat=technology accessed on 17 Apr 08 Mr. Rajeev Kumar, Organisational Communication in Corporate Restructuring – a metaphorical analysis ofdownsizing organisations,abstract,

http://www.tiss.edu/Rajeev.pdf   accessed on 25 May 08.

http://www.businessballs.com/ethical_management_leadership.htm accessed on 18 May 08.

http://www.thefreedictionary.com/ethics   accessed on 18 May 08.

http://en.wikipedia.org/wiki/Ethics   Accessed on 18 may 08. David Smith and Louise Drudy, Corporate Culture and Organisational Ethics, © Springer. Part of Springer Science+Business Media

http://www.springerlink.com/content/nq648l23118m1k85/   accessed on 18 May 08. N. Purnima Srikrishna http://www.hinduonnet.com/jobs/0802/2008022050060700.htm   accessed on 18 May 08.

Mary Gormandy , Whitehttp://business.lovetoknow.com/wiki/A_Definition_for_Business_Ethics   accessed on 18 May 08.

http://www.thelaborers.net/constitutions/ETHICS_definition.htm accessed on 18 May 08.

http://www.freeessays.cc/db/20/egn28.shtml   accessed on 18 May 08.

http://www.soi.org/reading/change/culture.shtml   accessed on 19 May 08.

http://www.culture-at-work.com/concept2.html   accessed on 19 May 08.

http://dictionary.bnet.com/definition/Corporate+Culture.html   accessed on 19 May 08.

http://www.answers.com/topic/culture   accessed on 19 May 08. Susan M. Heathfield, Culture: Your Environment for People at Work

http://humanresources.about.com/od/organizationalculture/a/culture_2.htm accessed on 19 May 08. 'WORK CULTURE IN INDIA' Published by hunk007rvs under INTERVIEW, PLACEMENT QUESTION, good, infosys paper, internet, microsoft, social community, tcs

http://hunk007rvs.blog.co.in/tag/work-culture-in-india/   accessed on 27 Jul 08. Kaur, Pritam, WORK CULTURE, Nursing Journal of India, May 2004

http://findarticles.com/p/articles/mi_qa4036/is_200405/ai_n9425691 accessed on 22 May 08.

http://www.confirmit.com/solutions/application/employee-satisfaction-survey.aspx   accessed on 12 May 08. Employee Satisfaction, Monday, September 11, 2006 http://dqindia.ciol.com/content/DQTop20_2006/ employers06/2006/106091101.asp   accessed on 12 May 08 Sarita Rani & TV Mahalingam, A DQ-IDC INDIA SURVEY: BPO Employee Satisfaction Survey 2003, Tuesday, October 21 2003.

http://dqindia.ciol.com/content/dqtop202k3/bpo/203102121.asp accessed on 12 May 08 Bob Piper, The Talon Group, Professional Builder Why Employee Satisfaction?,January 1, 2006,© 2008, Reed Business Information, a division of Reed Elsevier Inc. All Rights Reserved.

http://www.housingzone.com/probuilder/article/CA6296666.html accessed on 08 May 08. Lee W. Lee, Leadership,

http://www.answers.com/leadership&r=67   accessed on 25 May 08. Robert Heller, Effective Leadership: Mike Brearley's team management, 2006-07-08 21:18.

http://www.thinkingmanagers.com/management/effective-leadership.php accessed on 07/05/08 Marie G. McIntyre, Ph.D,.Building an Effective management Team,

http://www.yourofficecoach.com/Topics/building_an_effective_mgmt_ team.htm   accessed on 07/05/08

http://www.cliffsnotes.com/WileyCDA/CliffsReviewTopic/Types-of-Teams.topicArticleId-8944,articleId-8901.html   accessed on 23May 08. Kenneth Crow,DRM Associates, BUILDING   EFFECTIVE PRODUCT DEVELOPMENT TEAMS / INTEGRATED PRODUCT TEAMS,195199tes use prohibited.

http://www.npd-solutions.com/pdt.html   accessed on 07/05/08 Rick Johnson, 10 Tips to Create an Effective Management Team,

http://ezinearticles.com/?10-Tips-to-Create-an-Effective-Management-Team&id=487349   accessed on 07/05/08 Susan M. Heathfield, Twelve Tips for Team Building: How to Build Successful Work Teams, How to Make Teams Effective.

http://humanresources.about.com/od/involvementteams/a/twelve_ tip_team.htm   accessed on 07/05/08 Sandra G Leggat, Effective healthcare teams require effective team members: defining teamwork competencies,School of Public Health, La Trobe University, Victoria,

3086, Australia' 07 February 2007,

http://www.biomedcentral.com/1472-6963/7/17#   accessed on 07/05/08

http://en.wikipedia.org/wiki/Stakeholder_(corporate) accessed on 30 May 08. Military power projection, From Wikipedia, the free encyclopedia,

http://en.wikipedia.org/wiki/Power_projection   accessed on 23 May 08. Political power,From Wikipedia, the free encyclopedia,

http://en.wikipedia.org/wiki/Political_power   accessed on 23 May 08. Decision making, From Wikipedia, the free encyclopedia, http://en.wikipedia.org/wiki/   accessed on 23 May 08 Decision Making Techniques, How to Make Good

Decisions.http://www.mindtools.com/pages/main/newMN_TED.htm accessed on 23 May 08. Robert Harris, Introduction to Decision Making, Version Date: July 2, 1998,

http://www.virtualsalt.com/crebook5.htm accessed on 2 May 08.

http://www.thinkingmanagers.com/business-management/decision-making.php   accessed on 23 May 08.

http://www.businessballs.com/problemsolving.htm   accessed on 23 May 08. Paul, Turner, Organisational Communication The Role Of The Hr Professional BP Sinha & MN Reddy, Organisational Communication: A structural and Functional Analysis

http://www.bagchee.com/books.php?id=17651   accessed on 25 May 08. Ethical leadership, decision-making, and organizations

http://www.businessballs.com/ethical_management_leadership.htm accessed on 13/05/08

hhttp://en.wikipedia.org/ wiki/Love accessed on 22/01/0